Lavender

Lavender

HOW TO GROW AND USE
THE FRAGRANT HERB

Ellen Spector Platt

STACKPOLE
BOOKS

Copyright © 1999 by Ellen Spector Platt

Published by
STACKPOLE BOOKS
5067 Ritter Road
Mechanicsburg, PA 17055
www.stackpolebooks.com

Printed in China

10 9 8 7 6 5 4 3 2 1

FIRST EDITION

Cover design by Wendy Reynolds
Cover photograph by Ellen Spector Platt
Interior photographs by Ellen Spector Platt, unless otherwise noted

Library of Congress Cataloging-in-Publication Data

Platt, Ellen Spector.
    Lavender : how to grow and use the fragrant herb / Ellen Spector Platt. — 1st ed.
      p.   cm.
    Includes bibliographical references and index.
    ISBN 0–8117–2849–8
    1. Lavenders. 2. Lavenders—Utilization. I. Title.
SB317.L37P58 1999
635.9′3396—dc21   98–41973
                                                        CIP

For the Next Gardeners,
Niki, Laney, Emily, and Max

Contents

Acknowledgments

I am greatly indebted to my primary lavender spotters, those who trained their eyes to see a purple haze at 60 miles per hour or while distracted by traffic jams and city snarls and alerted me to fantastic photo opportunities: Anne and Alex Scott, Dolores Delin, Christine Gaffney, and as always, Ben Platt, who has the family eagle eye for discovering hidden treasures.

Thanks also to those generous souls who allowed me to photograph the special gardens that they worked so hard to achieve: Toni Groff, Joe Quesada, Louise and Cyrus Hyde at Well-Sweep Herb Farm, Barbara A. Steel at Alloway Creek Gardens and Herb Farm, Mary Vogel at Lavender Hedge, Pauline Pettitt-Palenik at Cool Spring Lavender Farm, and Ruth Flounders at Sculp's Hill Herbary. Those that welcome the public are listed in the back of the book under Lavender Sources (pages 107 and 108).

I appreciate beyond words the talents of the superb nature photographer and teacher Alan Rokach, whose comments resound in my ear every time I snap the shutter. He shares his knowledge, experience, and artistic eye in a generous way that forces all of his students to improve. And thanks to Christine Gaffney for her many creative contributions as assistant photo stylist.

Kyle Weaver, who has edited two of my books at Stackpole, has done so with unfailing grace, humor, and careful attention to detail. I am also grateful to Katherine Powis, librarian extraordinaire at the New York Horticultural Society, for pointing me always in the right direction.

Lavender Sweet Lavender

A whiff of an aroma recalls a childhood memory—the lavender man standing in front of Whitman's, the landmark Philadelphia confectionery shop, with snow white hair, ruddy pockmarked face, and around his neck a stout strap holding his tray. The tray is filled with lavender buds, violet-blue and redolent to passersby on their way to the glamorous shops of Chestnut Street. He sells his "lavender, sweet lavender, five a pack, six for a quarter" in small glassine envelopes. The lavender man supports himself on crutches, as he is missing one leg. He has claimed the same spot for years, always at Whitman's, where stylish women go to lunch or to savor butterscotch sundaes.

Other people have fond childhood memories of lavender. Some fifty years later, as I hang bunches of the fragrant flowers to sell at the Philadelphia Flower Show, women strolling by halt in their tracks as they catch the scent and wistfully recall, "When I was a girl . . ."

LEFT: *L. angustifolia* attracts butterflies and bees to the Cloisters Museum garden, typical of monastery gardens, where monks washed themselves and their clothes.

CHAPTER ONE

Lavender Varieties

Most sources list the Mediterranean area, Greece, France, Spain, and the North African coast as the native habitat of lavender, but several botanists think that India also may have been part of the native range. Romans used it to perfume and disinfect their baths and may have taken it to England when they moved north to conquer. It was one of the plants brought by colonists to America with other favored species to make the new world feel more like home.

The botanical name for lavender is *Lavandula,* its genus name, which comes from the Latin *lavandus,* "to be washed," or *lavare,* "to wash." Lavender is in the mint family, Labiatae, along with rosemary, mints, and sages, and displays the characteristic square stem, opposite leaves, and lipped corolla on the flower.

The taxonomy of lavender is confusing. The designations French, English, and Spanish are not botanical reference points and sometimes refer only to the country in which the lavenders are planted. Most of the varieties called English are of the species *angustifolia,* but this species is also planted in France. Because of such ambiguity, I don't refer to varieties by country name. I suggest you do the same and refuse to patronize a grower that can't help you by calling plants by their only proper name—the botanical one, consisting of the species in Latin and the variety name in English. Using the Latin names

LEFT: *L. a.* 'Premier' in a mixed perennial border at Well-Sweep Herb Farm in Port Murray, New Jersey.

may seem difficult, but you will be less confused in the long run, and if you are particular about what you plant, this is the only way to be accurate.

In regard to using a country name, however, there is one exception. 'Dutch' is a variety name of the *Lavandula x intermedia,* and a handsome variety it is too. 'Dutch' refers to one specific plant and is not a catchall for every lavender grown in the Netherlands.

Some of the hardy lavenders are known as lavandins. This name refers to the hybrid cross of *Lavandula angustifolia* and *L. latifolia,* which produces *L. x intermedia,* a lovely cross between the two parents with excellent characteristics of both. Since *Lavandula x intermedia* is a mouthful to say, the shortened version in garden-speak is lavandin. These plants generally bloom about one month later than the *angustifolias.*

Lavender has no known insect pests, but too much moisture causes root rot, and will kill the plant, as will radical pruning of old, woody plants. Plants in a favored location can live twenty to twenty-five years, but some commercial farms replace shrubs after five years of growth for the best oil production.

Flowers bloom in June, July, and August. Some species have a second, sparser bloom (about 25 percent of the first cutting) although some varieties have been bred to produce a larger second flush of bloom.

Because lavender is so easy for experts to pollinate, new varieties are offered to the public each year. In the February 1994 issue of *Herb Companion,* Kathleen Halloran reported thirty species and more than one hundred named varieties and cultivars. Plant breeders are constantly seeking better flower or foliage color, different growth habits, earlier or later bloom times, the ability to rebloom, greater hardiness, and especially, plants with combinations of the most desirable characteristics. Some varieties are hard to distinguish because differences such as hardiness or bloom time are not immediately apparent.

Some species grow readily from seed and are very easy to hybridize. The process of breeding a new variety is a time-demanding but simple concept. Start with a specific goal—for example, a lavender with deep pink flowers that will look pretty dried. Begin with a pink variety like *Lavandula angustifolia* 'Jean Davis'. Look at all of the 'Jean Davis' plants in flower; select the ones with the deepest color flowers, harvest the seed, and plant them. Plants should be isolated from other lavenders so that they are not cross-pollinated by insects. After they bloom, select the deepest pink plants from the first generation. Discard any plants with other undesirable characteristics. Harvest the seed and plant a second generation. Again, select the deepest pink, healthy-looking plants and discard the others. You now may want to hand-pollinate the plants with the deepest pink flowers, by touching pollen from the stamens to the top of the pistil of another flower on the same plant. A small paintbrush can be used to facilitate this process.

After six or eight generations from planting seed to maturing seed, the characteristics of the plant should be stabilized, and you should have plants of a reliable deep pink color. Although seed companies develop their own varieties in their breeding programs, they also rely on home gardeners who like to experiment to bring in seed they have developed in this way. After further testing and development, a seed company might choose to go into production with a new named variety that could even be named after you.

Is it really necessary to have a choice of so many varieties? I read of two new cultivars that look the same to the naked eye but are named differently

L. angustifolia is a popular hardy species, 1¹/₂ to 2 feet tall and an intense blue purple.

Lavender Hedge, a private garden near Philadelphia where Mary Vogel planted the striking combination of *L. a.* 'Croxton's Wild' with artemisia.

because they have different DNA, which is visible only under a high-powered microscope. This is perhaps of interest to botanists but irrelevant and confusing for the home gardener. Some varieties are very hard to find and may be available in only one nursery, but there probably are other varieties that will serve your purpose just as well and are more readily available. Determine the characteristics most important to you and start your selection there.

Factors to Consider in Selecting a Variety

Hardiness

Most lavenders are hardy to zone 5 and grow well in zones 5 through 8, though some varieties will grow in zones 9 and 10. Some gardeners grow lavender as a perennial with protection in zones 3 and 4. Hardiness to frost is not the only planting consideration, however. Although lavenders can take dry heat, they do not do well in high humidity. The American Horticultural Society has developed a new chart called the United States Plant Heat-Zone Map. It divides the country into twelve zones according to the average number of days on which the heat rises above 86 degrees F. The heat-zone guide is a companion to the better-known USDA map of horticultural zones divided according to average low temperatures. Since lavenders, like most plants, are affected by humid heat as well as frost, consulting both maps to find your frost and heat zones should tell you how well your plants will do.

Length of the Flowering Stem

If you want to sell fresh lavender to florists or retail at a farm stand, you must base your choice of variety first on length of flowering spike, second on sweet aroma, and only third on flower color. Foliage is less important here, since much of it will be stripped for the vase. For floral designers, stem length is critical, as clients typically pay more for a larger arrangement than for a small posy.

Height of the Shrub

In the garden, the height of the foliage may be more important than the length of the flower stems. If you are planting a low hedge in a traditional herb bed, one of the compact plants, such as 'Munstead', the pretty pink 'Jean Davis', or 'Dwarf Blue', which grows to 12 inches on mounds of gray foliage, may be your answer. For smaller plants, look for the appellation *nana*, Latin for "dwarf," in the botanical name. Plants may be described as "dwarf" or "compact" in catalogs. For taller plants in the annual border, I love the tender fernleaf lavender *(L. multifida)*. If you want a perennial hedge by a walkway, look for the tallest, hardiest variety you can find, perhaps *L.* x *intermedia* 'Grappenhall', with dark blue-purple blooms 40 inches high.

Color and Texture of Foliage

Foliage color and texture can be at least as important as flower color or more so, since the foliage is present for more months of the year than the flowers. Lavender foliage is particularly attractive. New shoots are a delicate green, and the foliage matures to gray-green *(L. stoechas)*, blue-green, or gray-white *(L. a.* 'Grey Lady'). *L. viridis* has chartreuse foliage and creamy yellow flowers. *L. lantana* 'Boiss' has woolly leaves. The tender varieties of *L. dentata* have deep green, fragrant leaves that are toothed on the edges and make fine winter pot plants. If you want a wide leaf with a definite presence of its own, consider one of the *intermedias*.

The Flower

If you examine a lavender flower closely, you will see that the petals, which make up the corolla, emerge from the bud, or calyx. Both the calyx and corolla are visible as the flower matures. If you plan to cut the flower spikes for drying, it's only the color of the calyx that matters. The petals don't dry well; they turn brown and fall off. The calyx is usually somewhat different in tone from the petals and should be as dark a color as possible for a beautiful dried flower.

If you want to dry the flowers for use in winter bouquets, a deep rich color is all important. For this purpose, I prefer *L. a.* 'Hidcote' or *L. x intermedia* 'Dutch'. I use 'Grosso' or 'Provence' when color is less important and the length of the flower spike is critical.

In the garden, white or pink lavender may surprise your visitors, as many people don't realize that these flowers come in colors other than lavender. White varieties often have *alba* in the botanical name. Popular pink varieties are *L. a.* 'Jean Davis' and 'Lodden Pink'. Don't expect white or pink lavender to dry to a pretty shade.

For a child's garden, plant *L. pedunculata* (also listed as *L. stoechas pedunculata*), which has petals that stand well above the flower heads and look like butterfly wings. This is a tender plant, so if you live north of zone 8, plant it in a pot in the garden and bring it inside during the winter. This variety is sometimes called Spanish lavender, but beware, as there are other varieties also called Spanish lavender that don't have the large wings.

Flowering Schedule

Lavender is usually considered a summer-blooming flower, but don't expect too much from new seedlings the first year in which you grow or buy the plant. By the second year, you will have a nice, showy plant. If you are designing a garden where time of bloom is important, *L. a.* 'Tucker's Early Purple' gives you a head start in the garden. *L. angustifolia* 'Irene Doyle' (or 'Two Seasons'), 'Pastor's Pride', 'Sharon Roberts', and 'Buena Vista' have all been bred to give a strong second flush of growth in the fall. In general, the *angustifolias* bloom about three weeks before the *intermedias* in my zone 5 garden. If you want an early variety, ask the horticulturist at your local garden center or herb farm.

Species and Common Varieties

Lavandula angustifolia

L. angustifolia is sometimes also called English lavender, true lavender, *L. vera,* or *L. officinalis. Angustifolia* means "narrow-leaved." This species contains many varieties, which all have a sweet fragrance and flower heads appearing on one short spike. Most will flower from seed in two years.

'Alba': white flowers, stems 20 inches long, flower spikes 2 to 3 inches.

'Buena Vista': bred for sweet fragrance, long flower heads of deep lavender, blooms in June and September.

'Compacta': light purple, 1^1/$_2$ feet high, compact form.

'Graves': very tall for this species and productive, 2^1/$_2$ to 3 feet, good fresh or dried.

The hardy lavender 'Jean Davis' has pink flowers but bright white buds that light up a spring garden.

L. x *intermedia* 'Grosso' greening up in early spring makes a strong showing of foliage. The flowers bloom pale blue-gray on tall stems.

'Grey Lady': 18-inch bloom height on compact plants, gray foliage, lavender-blue flowers; use for edging.

'Hidcote': plant 16 inches; dark purple-blue flower a favorite for deep color when dried; sweet, strong scent.

'Irene Doyle': dark purple flower, blooms both early and late, semidwarf, 9-inch foliage height, 6-inch flower stems.

'Jean Davis': 18-inch bloom height, bright white in bud, pink in bloom, blooms turn grayish when dried, early bloomer, very hardy and strong scented, excellent for formal knot garden.

'Lady': 15-inch flower height, 12-inch spread, hardy to zone 5; may bloom from seed the first year, three to six months, depending on climate; bred for early bloom from selections of 'Munstead'; slow to spread.

'Lodden Blue': semidwarf plants of 15 inches with 6- to 8-inch flower spikes; RHS award of merit.

'Lodden Pink': plant to 17 1/2 inches, pink flowers.

'Munstead': plant 14 inches, a favorite for small edges to define herb gardens; early bloomer, lilac-colored flowers, sweet fragrance.

'Nana Alba': dwarf 8-inch plant, short spikes, white flowers, and silver foliage.

'Pastor's Pride': dark lavender blooms, good rebloom if first flower spikes are all removed from plant.

'Rosea': 15-inch soft pink flowers.

'Royal Velvet': dark purple, velvety flowers.

'Sachet': heady perfume.

'Sharon Roberts': good rebloom if spent flowers are removed, dark lavender flowers, vigorous.

'Susan Belsinger': dark purple flower, blooms both early and late, 7-inch plant height.

'Twickel Purple': compact plant, 2 to 3 feet, green leaves sometimes flushed with purple, flowers on long spikes in a fanlike cluster, blooms after 'Munstead'.

Lavandula latifolia

L. latifolia is commonly called spike lavender or just spike. *Latifolia* means "broad-leaved," and these plants have leaves that are broader and grayer than those of *L. angustifolia*. *L. latifolia* also has taller flower spikes than the *angustifolias*, deep gray leaves, bright blue flowers, and a camphorous odor rather than a sweet smell. Axial shoots grow from the main flower stem. It propagates easily from seed. Numerous crosses between *L. latifolia* and *L. angustifolia*, called *L. x intermedia*, or lavandin, are prized for their appearance, aroma, and hardiness.

Lavandula x intermedia

Lavandula x intermedia is more tolerant of high humidity than *L. angustifolia*. These species usually don't set seed and must be propagated from cuttings.

'Abrialli': popular in France, large flower head, excellent dried.

L. dentata is added to this commercial planting on a fashionable boulevard in Madrid. The toothed edges of the leaves inspired the name of this species.

'Dutch': dark purple flower 16-inch foliage height with 20-inch flower spikes, blooms early to midseason.

'Fred Boutin': pale violet flowers, 16-inch foliage height, 20-inch flower spikes, blooms midseason, vigorous.

'Giant Hidcote': strong scent and early bloom, lavender-blue flowers, large flower heads on long spikes.

'Grappenhall': 40-inch bloom height, early bloomer, dark purple-blue flower, wide gray leaf.

'Grosso': 30-inch bloom height, blue-violet flower, violet-gray when dried, very fragrant, also called fat spike.

'Melissa': pink flowers, good for sachet.

'Provence': one of the tallest varieties, named for lavender-growing region of France, strong scent.

'Provence, White Form' (*L.* x *intermedia* 'Alba'): compact at 12 inches.

'Seal': dark purple flower, bloom height 3 to 4 inches, blooms early to midseason.

Lavandula dentata

L. dentata species are sometimes called French lavenders, but so are *L. stoechas.* These are tender species, with toothed leaves and short flower heads on long stems.

L. d. variegata: foliage has creamy variegation.

'Goodwin Creek Grey': long bloom period, silvery leaves, deep purple corollas, excellent for topiaries or containers.

The flower of *L. dentata* is delicate and lovely in the garden but not useful for drying.

Other Species

Lavandula lanata are tender species that have a balsam scent, woolly leaves, and deep purple corollas. Not good for wet, humid climates.

Lavandula viridis species have tender, very fragrant chartreuse leaves and white flowers. Plant grows to 39 inches.

L. lanata, a tender lavender, has silvery leaves with a woolly texture and dislikes high humidity.

L. stoechas (dwarf form) spreads its butterfly wings in the fabulous gardens of Wave Hill in the Bronx, New York. Children—and their parents—love it.

Lavandula stoechas is a tender species sometimes called 'Spanish'. Flowers on short stems, fat purple bracts on top, not good for decorative drying.

Lavandula stoechas pedunculata, also called Spanish lavender, is a tender lavender that must be wintered indoors in zone 5. Height and spread of 24 inches. Large, purple bracts on top of flower spikes look like butterfly wings or rabbit ears. Not for drying. Gray-green foliage.

The tender downy lavender *(L. multifida)* stays in a pot year-round, in summer residing next to the daylily 'Stella d'Oro', in winter on a sunporch.

Downy lavender *(L. multifida)*, though tender, continues to bloom in October even after two light frosts.

Lavandula multifida, or downy lavender, has ferny leaves. Plant grows to 2 feet and flower stems to 2 to 3 feet tall. Flower spike is in three parts, resembling a pitchfork. The flowers continue to bloom in my garden through October despite five or six nights of temperatures just below freezing. Not recommended for decorative drying because the flower color changes quickly from blue to brown.

CHAPTER TWO

History of Lavender

Folklore about lavender begins in ancient times, when the plant that grew wild on the rocky shores of the Mediterranean was used by Roman soldiers to perfume their bath water. English lavender soaps and bath products are a favorite tourist purchase, but lavender likely was one of the many imports of the Roman soldiers who invaded England in the second century B.C.

The Greek physician Pedanius Dioscordes, writing in the years 40 to 70 A.D., produced a volume *De Materia Medica*, which was widely quoted up through the seventeenth century for its botanical wisdom. Of lavender, he says, "the decoction of lavender is like Hyssop, good for griefs in the thorax. It is also mingled profitably with the Antidotes."

Before Linnaeus, who systematized botanical names, plants growing in different parts of the world, and indeed in different centuries, were often confused. Plants were named differently in different languages, and the inconsistency made for errors. For example, some think that lavender is the spikenard referred to in the Bible, and others believe it's a completely different species.

Before the advent of pharmaceutical companies, which developed and standardized medicines, there were healers who used natural plants to effect cures. In the middle ages in Europe, growing herbs was a function of the

LEFT: The Cloisters branch of the Metropolitan Museum of Art, New York, complements its famous collection of art and architecture of the Middle Ages with plants growing within three separate cloistered gardens typical of that time.

monasteries. The cloisters of such societies were divided into the kitchen garden, in which grew fruits, vegetables, and cooking herbs, and the infirmarian's garden, in which grew the healing herbs. Certain monks or nuns were assigned to plant a physick garden and gathered leaves, berries, flowers, and roots from the fields and woods and dried and stored them for later use. Later this task fell to the lady of the manor, who would grow and store herbs and dose her household and the poor surrounding her. These skills were part of her girlhood education. From these herbs she made "simples" to keep in her still room, remedies coming from plants thought to have particular virtues. Turner, in his sixteenth-century *Herball,* recommends that "the flowers of Lavender quilted in a cappe and dayly worne are good for all diseases of the head that come of a cold cause and they comfort the braine very well" (translated into English by John Goodyear in 1655 and quoted by Joseph Krutch in his *Herbal).*

In the Cloisters herb garden, lavender is paired with Our Lady's bedstraw *(Galium vernum)* and more than 250 other species cultivated during the Middle Ages.

Laundresses in medieval England were referred to as "lavenders" because of both the old Roman custom of washing clothes in lavender water and the Latin term *lavare,* meaning "to wash." The poorest women who were lavenders had the reputation of being prostitutes, and dire warnings were written about association with them. An anonymous poet in the early 1500s wrote, "Thou shalt be my lavender (laundress)/to wash and keep clean all my gear/Our two beds shall be set/without any let."

The German nun Hildegard of Bingen (1098–1179) was educated in a convent and entered the Benedictine order, where she later became abbess. Although she was called a

saint, she was never formally canonized. Known for her musical composi-
tions, treatment of the sick, healing powers, and miraculous cures, she advo-
cated the use of lavender water, a decoction of vodka, gin, or brandy mixed
with lavender, for migraines.

Lavender was thought to be remarkably effective against apoplexy, palsy
and loss of speech. "It profiteth them much that have the palsey if they be
washed with the distilled water from the lavender flowers or are anointed with
the oil made from the flowers and olive oil in such manner as oil of roses is
used," said the barber-surgeon John Gerard in his 1597 *Herbal.* To cure
headaches, *Lavandula stoechas* was mixed with other herbs and worn in a little bag around the neck—a red silk bag for noblemen and a muslin bag for
commoners. Salmon reported in his 1710 *Herbal* that "it is good against the
bitings of serpents, mad-dogs and other venomous creatures."

The effectiveness of lavender and other herbs as remedies for various ailments remains in dispute to this day, and there's no telling how often cures
have resulted from a placebo effect, or the *belief* that the herb is healing rather
than the herb itself.

Lavender also has a place in the superstitions of some cultures. In 1912,
Lady Northcote wrote in her *Book of Herb Lore* that in Spain and Portugal,
lavender was used as a strewing herb on the floors of churches and was tossed
into bonfires to avert evil spirts on St. John's Day. In Tuscany, an old custom
was to pin sprigs of lavender on children's shirts to avert the evil eye.
Although my friend from Milano scoffs at this superstition as a peasant custom, she admits that she would never wear a lavender- or violet-colored dress
to the opening of the opera or theater, because people in the cast might think
she was trying to jinx the performance. She laughs when I try to delve further
into the origins of this notion and says that it just isn't done, in the way that
in the United States not so long ago, you would never wear black to a wedding
because the bride and her family might object to the symbolism of mourning.

CHAPTER THREE

Uses of Lavender

The leaves, stems, buds, and flowers of lavender all contain essential oils, and all are valuable for different purposes. The parts of the plant can be used fresh, dried, or distilled with the essential oils extracted. Certainly the flowers are more esthetically pleasing than the stems, but if I were stitching sachets where the aromatic stuffing would be hidden to the observer, I would make my meager crop go farther by using finely chopped bits of stems and leaf along with the flowers.

Making essential oil is not usually a project for the home gardener, as you must first construct a distilling apparatus and you need tons of lavender and large-scale tilling and harvesting equipment for commercial purposes. At the Norfolk Lavender Farm in England, 500 pounds of flowers are used to produce 1 1/2 pounds of oil, which then ages for at least a year. For highest-quality oil, the flower spikes are cut when the buds are just starting to open, and the flowers are stripped from the stems to be processed. Flowers need to be spread out to dry rapidly but kept from the sun after picking so that less of the oils will evaporate into the air. Distillation should occur within a week to prevent additional loss of strength. Distilling involves placing the stripped flowers over a vat of boiling water and collecting the oil in copper tubing as it is released and condenses.

LEFT: **Products scented with lavender include soaps, bath salts, sleep masks, eau de toilette, and air fresheners.**

Various sources state with certainty that the best oil comes from flowers grown in England; others report just as adamantly that the best oil comes from flowers grown in the south of France. The best oil is made from the buds or from fully opened flowers, depending on whom you listen to. One thing is sure—as with fine wines, the quality of the oil varies from season to season, depending on the weather, the age of the plants, and the soil. Although there are lavender farms in the United States that sell their products commercially, the quantity of flowers required is a problem. A small group of flower farmers in Washington state have found a seemingly practical solution by forming a co-op that will purchase a mobile still that can travel among the farms, making the enterprise profitable for all.

You can buy plants, dried bunches, dried buds, and small vials of oil from the sources listed on pages 107 and 108. When it comes to the essential oils, know the reliability of your sources. There are synthetic products masquerading as the real thing, and diluted oils listed as pure.

Before taking lavender internally—for cooking or medicinal purposes—be sure that it hasn't been treated with pesticides by the growers. The best way to be sure is to grow your own, or know your source to be reliable. Much of the dried lavender available commercially is of potpourri quality, not cooking or medicinal quality.

Aromatic Uses

Where lavender grows in abundance, linens are still draped over the small shrubs to dry. The evaporating oils infuse the linens with fragrance. Imagine a closetful of sheets, warm from the sun and redolent with the aroma of lavender.

The sweet, pungent oil of lavender is found in every part of the plant, but it is mostly the essential oil in the flower that is distilled for use in perfumes, potpourris, sachets, soaps, and bath oils. Though it is impractical for home gardeners to distill their own essential oil, you can make a simple lavender oil. with a high-quality almond or olive oil. Fill a covered jar loosely with lavender stems, including both leaves and flowers, lightly bruised between the fingers. Pour in oil to the top; let the fresh or dried lavender steep for about a month, shaking the jar daily. Strain through cheesecloth and, using a funnel, decant into a clean bottle or covered jar. Add stems of lavender with flowers for decoration. Lavender oil produced in this way makes a lovely massage oil with soothing and relaxing properties.

Some of the more pungent species of lavender that have a camphorous smell are hung in bundles or made into sachets to repel moths and flies. Try *L. multifida* (downy lavender) or *L. stoechas* tied together with tansy plus southernwood or wormwood as a moth repellent for woolens.

Although you can purchase ceramic vaporizing rings to put around a lightbulb, one drop of oil dabbed directly on the bulb releases fragrance every time you turn on the lamp. You can simmer lavender, alone or in combinations with other herbs and spices, in a small electric potpourri pot for aroma throughout the house. I prefer to use a small saucepan, simmering on a back burner of the stove, with water and whatever herbs and spices I'm in the mood for. In winter, for a cheery fragrance, I simmer lavender with cloves, cinnamon, and nutmeg (either whole or ground); strips of orange, lemon, or grapefruit rind; and a few small pinecones with enough water to cover well, adding more water as needed and watching that the pot doesn't boil dry.

Pauline Pettitt-Palenik of Cool Spring Lavender Farm sprinkles lavender buds

A public garden in Toledo, Spain, features a post proclaiming "Peace to all mankind" in four languages. A lavender hedge draws the viewer's eye to the post.

directly onto her carpets. Crushing by foot traffic releases the aromas. This practice will help eliminate pet odors and impart a lovely scent to the room. When vacuuming, the buds get taken up by the sweeper and disperse the scent throughout the room. Don't try this with your antique oriental rugs, however, lest the oils harm the colors and the fabric over time.

Medicinal Uses

An accurate medical diagnosis should precede any self-treatment with lavender or any other herb. And since even small quantities of some essential oils can be toxic, you must know what you are doing. Unfortunately, some people believe that if one drop is good, ten drops will be ten times better, with disastrous consequences. An experienced and knowledgeable herbal practitioner can be of help if you want to experiment with herbal remedies.

The aroma of lavender is said to have soothing properties that will relieve stress and help you sleep. Five to ten drops in a warm bath before sleep is soothing to the nerves, and several drops of essential oil on the temples may alleviate or cure a headache. The oil is absorbed by the skin. The oil may be effective because some chemical components help slow nerve impulses, reducing nervousness and excitability and thus inducing sleep. Try making a mask filled with lavender buds to place over the eyes when drifting off to sleep or just for relaxation purposes.

Although lavender has soothing properties, it is a circulatory and uterine stimulant, and lavender teas should be avoided during pregnancy. In particular, the *L. stoechas* seem to have stimulant properties.

Lavender is an ancient analgesic and some still use it for bug bites, mild burns, and skin irritation, rubbing it on the skin to relieve itching and reduce swelling. When out in the garden, pluck a few stems of the plant and rub directly on your exposed skin. In my garden, lavender, along with pennyroyal and wormwood, keeps us free from gnats, midges, and mosquitoes as we work. Herbalists keep pure essential lavender oil in the first-aid kit and use a drop or two on a cotton swab to wipe over burns, insect bites, and minor infections. James A. Duke in *The Green Pharmacy* recommends keeping a vial of lavender oil alongside your aloe for rubbing on burns in the kitchen. Colleen K. Dodt, in *The Essential Oils Book,* suggests using ten drops of lavender oil with 4 ounces of water in a spray bottle for sunburn relief.

Since lavender oil is soluble in alcohol, "lavender water" has been used for centuries as a restorative and as a tonic against weakness, fainting, and giddiness. This is a mixture of brandy, wine, or vodka with a few drops of lavender oil, sometimes diluted with water, and sometimes not. Clearly, the alcohol content is potent enough on its own, and it is unclear exactly what effects the lavender adds.

Cleansing

Use five to ten drops of essential oil poured directly into bath water just before entering the tub, to aid in cleansing and to wash the hair. Some believe it kills head lice and that it has antiseptic, antibacterial, and antifungal properties. It has also been used as a treatment for acne, probably because of its antiseptic properties.

If you have lavender from the garden and want to use it directly in the bath, tie up small bunches, leaves included, in old knee-high stockings, small squares of cheesecloth, or other loosely woven fabric. Squeeze the bag several times to release the oils just before you throw it into the readied bath. I once tried throwing the herbs directly into the tub without a wrapping. I emerged thirty minutes later with leaves and blossoms clinging to my skin, like a mermaid from the sea.

A new cosmetic product is "body tea," herbs packed in a small bag for dangling in a hot bath. Several packages of body teas make lovely small gifts, bundled in decorative netting, accompanied by a note with an explanation of use, and tied with a ribbon.

Lavender oil can also be used as a household cleaner. Try ten to twenty drops of oil in your scrub water for your regular cleaning jobs, from floors to counters to bathrooms.

Flavoring

The flavor of lavender is intense, and as with other spices, don't overdo it; too much lavender can overwhelm the palate and taste bitter. Small amounts are used to flavor sorbets, sugars, teas, jellies, vinegars, stews, and baked goods.

Diluted lavender oil is used in gargles and to mask the flavors of unpleasant pharmaceuticals. Don't use more than a few drops of concentrated oil, however; as with almost all medicines, too strong a dose may be poisonous.

CHAPTER FOUR

Lavender in the Garden

Kitchen Herbs

Lavender is rather new to the kitchens of fine cooks in the United States, and many folks are still reluctant to try it. It was in the fine French restaurant L'Absinthe in Manhattan that I was first treated to a lavender sorbet atop a paper-thin open-faced apple tart. The chef explained that in the south of France, where he was raised, lavender was commonly used in cooking.

Surprise visitors to your kitchen herb garden by planting one of the sweet lavenders among the basil, thyme, oregano, lovage, borage, and coriander. After you explain that lavender is in the mint family and is closely related to rosemary, the concept will make sense, even to those who don't have a green thumb.

Once the lavender is planted in the kitchen herb bed, the next step is to incorporate it into your cooking. Some people are reluctant to try something flavored with lavender, because the idea seems too unusual. Often I don't tell my guests a recipe contains lavender until after I've received compliments on the delicate and unusual flavoring of a dish.

For years I stubbornly ignored the sage advice to plant cooking herbs as close to the kitchen door as sun and space allow. All my herbs were planted in my raised beds 500 feet from the kitchen. At suppertime, when the fish needed a few sprigs of dill or the chicken cried out for fresh rosemary, I fought

LEFT: Sam the cat basks amid the relaxing fragrance of Ruth Flounder's herb garden. Informal hedges are a popular use of lavender.

with myself to make that long trip out to the garden. Often my lazy side won out, and it was garlic again or, worse yet, a miserable sprinkling of some dried herbs I've had in my spice drawer for years, with a label from a supermarket long since bought out by another chain. I realize this is a shocking confession from someone in the flower and herb business, but it's true.

I've since seen the light and have reformed my ways, and now I have just enough plants near my kitchen for regular daily use. Even after the lavender has been harvested in early July for all my drying needs, there are sprigs pushing forth in a sparse second bloom, certainly enough to add to a fresh fruit dessert or sprinkle in my stew pot. Well into November, even after several light frosts, I can pick enough cooking lavender to flavor the pot.

Don't hesitate to put your cooking herbs in any sunny, convenient location, tucked here and there in your annual bed or perennial border or planted in containers. A few plants of your favorite herbs are all you need to perk up

The formal knot garden at Well-Sweep Herb Farm includes sheared plantings of lavender, germander, dwarf hyssop, and 'Red Pigmy' barberry.

your meals. If you prefer to plant a formal kitchen herb garden, see the discussion below on knot gardens.

Medicinal Gardens

Throughout history, the garden was often a metaphor for healing of the mind and spirit, as well as the body, and contained important herbs, such as foxglove for heart problems, poppy for killing pain, chamomile for sleep and relaxation, hyssop for coughs and chest ailments, and garlic, chives, and other alliums for purifying the blood. Lavender was planted for its antiseptic, carminative, and relaxing properties.

When planting an herb garden of medicinal plants, accurate labeling is extremely helpful to visitors, not just the common and botanical names, but an indication of the historical uses and which parts of the plant, such as root, leaves, flower, seeds, pods, or sap, were used, as well as what kind of preparation: a tea or infusion, salve, poultice, or plaster.

Again, some herbs can be dangerous if continuously used. It's important to learn about the effects of the herbs you grow for consumption or to ask a qualified herbalist before dosing yourself from the garden.

Knot and Foursquare Gardens

A formal herbal knot garden or a foursquare geometric garden is a thing of beauty, admired especially by those who do not have the temperament for carefully plotting, trimming, and manicuring. In a knot garden, the knot of herbs that weaves in and out seems to have no beginning and no end and is a botanical expression of infinity, used in Roman, Islamic, and medieval Christian cloistered gardens. The knot garden became increasingly popular during the Renaissance in England, along with larger planting of hedges in maze form. The knot garden not only is lovely to view while strolling but also is an intriguing sight also a window or balcony above. One of the dwarf hardy lavenders like 'Munstead' is particularly useful as a low hedge in a knot garden, a more fragrant and interesting alternative to boxwood or germander. The gray-green leaves add a subtle hint of color both before and after the bloom period, and the humming of the bees attracted to the flowers adds an aural note.

Another view of the formal knot garden at Well-Sweep Herb Farm.

In foursquare gardens, plantings are done in four squares or rectangles, with brick or gravel walkways forming a cross separating the squares and a focal point like a fountain, statue, or sundial in the center. Each of the quadrants is bordered by a low hedge. A dwarf lavender is a lovely plant for the edging, or one of the taller *angustifolias* or *intermedias* for the center of the square.

Problems inevitably arise when one of the plants in such a garden dies. Running to the nursery to buy a new plant is hardly the answer; the replacement always looks just like what it is—a poor substitute for the original. It's very hard to find fully grown replacements to fill in a hole in a seven-year-old hedge.

One serious gardener I know solves this problem by always starting with more plants than she needs. She plants the extra herbs in a specially prepared waiting bed off to one side of the garden and behind some shrubbery. When the need arises, usually several years after the patterned garden is planted, she has understudies of the same age, size, and variety ready to make their way onto the main stage.

Fragrance and Other Sensory Enhancements for the Garden

I had just moved into an 1830s stone farmhouse when I first happened upon the notion of a fragrance garden planted beneath a window. The idea was that the mingled perfumes of the garden bed would waft into the house through the open window. I was a novice gardener, and I planted heirloom peonies, fragrant iris, lavender, mock orange, and phlox, dreaming of future pleasures.

The original windows of my home, with their rippled glass windowpanes, have no sash mechanisms to hold up the heavy frames. Once the windows are raised, they must be propped up with dowel sticks, which I've painted to match each room. Though the 22-inch-thick stone walls provide wonderful insulation on a hot summer day, they also make the windowsills 20 inches deep. To get the proper leverage to raise the windows, I must hop up on the sills and raise straight up, not the most convenient activity. Where I live in northeastern Pennsylvania, most of the windows get propped up in June and closed in October. The peonies, iris, and mock orange have long since finished their bloom before the windows are open so that I can enjoy the fragrance. The lesson to be learned: Pay attention to bloom time. Select plants with a sequence of bloom that you can enjoy for at least eight months of the year.

Plant a fragrance garden where you will enjoy the benefits: late-spring- and summer-blooming plants around a patio; earlier fragrant plants on a path or at the entranceway, where you can enjoy the perfume coming and going. Plant creeping thyme between the flagstones that you tread upon entering and leaving your home. Include a bed of narcissus varieties and hyacinths early in the season, some lavenders like *L. angustifolia* or *L.* x *intermedia,* lily of the valley, a well-behaved mint like mountain mint *(Pycnanthemum pilosum),* summer lilies like rubrums, scented geraniums or lemon verbena, a fragrant heliotrope, peonies, bee balm, roses, and for late appeal, sweet Annie *(Artemisia annua).*

Modern cultivars of certain traditionally sweet-smelling flowers such as peonies, roses, and sweet peas have been bred for characteristics like disease resistance, size, and color, to the detriment of aroma. When ordering from a catalog or buying from a nursery when plants are not in bloom, make sure that the advertising copy or label includes a notation about the aroma, or you will be in for an unhappy surprise: visual beauty without the characteristic scent.

Enhance the sensory theme of your fragrance garden by including plants specifically for texture, like the velvety lamb's ear and the surprisingly dry

The carefree shrub rose 'Royal Bonica' makes a wonderful companion to most any other plant, such as this fourteen-year-old 'Hidcote'.

strawflower. Podded flowers like annual poppy, okra, nigella, and martynia add interest to a textural garden. Also consider sounds in the garden. Where scents are most powerful, the humming of bees will be evident. Add a simple water fountain or bubbling pump for pleasant, soothing sounds.

Hedges

Whether bordering a formal herb design, a path to the front door, or a walk-way leading into an outdoor garden room, lavender hedges are a traditional way of leading a visitor down the path. Because of the nature of its woody stems, lavender is more like a small shrub than a perennial, with the added advantage that the leaves remain on the plant during the winter. Some gardeners like to clip and trim the branches to a more regular shape; others allow the plants to sprawl, hanging over the path, where stray shoots get trodden on, releasing the most delightful odor.

In Manhattan, a vest-pocket park open to the public twenty-four hours a day features impeccable hedges of lavender and boxwood, with accents of purple petunias and silver artemisia.

The imposing building of the Madrid Archeology Museum in Spain is densely planted with hedges of lavender and gray santolina.

The lavender border at Well-Sweep Herb Farm displays a broad sampling of the cultivars they sell. The *angustifolias* were blooming in mid-June; the *intermedias* will bloom about a month later.

Attracting Butterflies

Butterflies love a jumble of colorful flowers, particularly tubular ones like lavender. They seem to be attracted to profusion, so if you want a butterfly garden, plant masses of flowers together.

Butterflies lay their eggs on specific host plants, which the hatched caterpillers use for food. Though lavender is not a major host plant, its nectar attracts butterflies, and since butterflies spread their wings in summer, the later blooming lavenders are perfect for northern gardens. Remember that pesticides are often fatal to butterflies, and herbicides cut down on many of the native habitats that butterflies seem to prefer.

In Mary Vogel's garden, lavender is everywhere, here in a mixed border with coral bells.

Mixed Perennial Borders

Lavender takes its place in a perennial border or mixed bed of perennials, annuals, and shrubs as much for its habit and foliage as for the flowers. Since the foliage stays on year-round, there is some presence in the border from the earliest days of spring through the following winter. The often grayish hue complements the hottest fuchsia or orange as well as pastel pinks, blues, and yellows. Even if you pick the flower spikes to use indoors, the plant still looks interesting for most of the year.

Because healthy lavender needs good air circulation as well as full sun, leave some room for the plants to spread; the larger lavenders may grow 5 to 6 feet across and don't enjoy the crowding of a typical mixed border.

Rock Gardens

Lavender in its native range, along the dry, rocky Mediterranean coast, grew in hot sun, poor soil with good drainage, and drought conditions. Rock gardens as they are designed in the United States resemble such habitat. They are usually located on steep embankments where the soil is shallow and the drainage excellent. Because of the slope, lavender plants are naturals for a south-facing rock garden. They are semi-drought tolerant and crave sunshine, and the protection of the slope will help ensure a long, happy life in horticultural zones 5 to 9.

A rock garden that pleases the eye repeats creeping and mounding forms, as well as colors, along its expanse, so it's good to use a number of plants of the same variety here and there throughout the garden.

Commercial Landscaping

Traveling through Spain with lavender on my mind, I expected to see purple drifts of Spanish lavender, growing wild on the hillside and planted in farmer's fields. They may well be there, but in two weeks of traveling I sighted none. Instead, lavender was used in commercial landscaping, from the few rocky beds surrounding a car rental lot in the Granada airport to mixed beds of *L. dentata* in front of an office building on a fashionable street in Madrid. The most impressive sight was the use of lavender in planters on the balconies of an insurance building on a bustling Madrid street. As seen by passersby on

An insurance office building in Madrid features an eye-stopping display of lavender.

Lavender and vines draping the balconies lend softness to the stark modern architecture.

A commercial building looks less sterile with planters of lavender and other foliage over-flowing from the balconies.

the ground, the purple haze repeated on all seven stories and on all four sides. The countless flower spikes were reflected into the mirrored facade, where they mingled with the reflections of the clouds above.

Container Plantings

In years gone by, I planted tender lavenders in my zone 5 flower border, watched them grow and bloom, and mourned their death with the first killing frost, around the middle of October. I now plant my *L. dentata* and *L. stoechas* in terra-cotta pots that sit on my patio near an old well pump from May to October. Their winter home is my sunporch, with a bright eastern exposure and sky-lights, where they flourish for the next six months, some blooming their fool heads off and some sending out the occasional bloom, which is cherished all

The sunny, dry climate of Santa Rosa County, California, supports a commercial lavender planting at the Matanzas Creek Winery. PHOTO BY SANDRA MACIVER.

My tender lavender *(L. dentata)* must spend its Pennsylvania winters on the sun-porch to avoid the icy winters. Taken out again in spring, it will survive many years.

the more when a heavy frost or dusting of snow coats the meadow just beyond the patio. The flowers are much paler indoors than out, almost white.

It's best to plant your tender varieties directly in containers, to avoid transplant shock every fall and spring, but if you haven't thought of that in time and still want to winter over indoors, you can dig the plants in late summer and transplant them into pots 2 to 3 inches wider than the root balls. Water well and leave outside for at least two weeks. Bring the pots indoors to their winter location before the heat goes on in the house, to reduce the additional shock of a drastic change in atmosphere. Though the plants might prefer 40- to 50-degree temperatures at night and 60 degrees during the day, most people don't have a separate conservatory in which to pamper their lavenders. I consider them part of the family and treat them like everyone else, with temperatures at 62 during the day, 60 at night, and 68 if I'm sitting for a long time reading or playing bridge. Water your container-grown lavenders when the top of the soil is dry to the touch, and use your favorite plant fertilizer about every three weeks.

Outdoors in late spring and summer, you can mix the plantings in the container with colorful annuals like pansies or dwarf lemon yellow marigolds. When the summer heat gets to be too much for the pansies, replace them with a delicate verbena or trailing nasturtium. Or plant one container full of lavender and other containers each filled with its own species. You can rearrange the pots as they come into their best bloom seasons. If you plant a container solely with lavender, you avoid a bare look in the pot, as many annuals die off when you bring the container inside to winter over.

The ability to plant lavender in containers means that those who have small spaces can enjoy this species on a terrace or patio or in a tiny yard and move the containers to better advantage throughout the season. Remember, though, that lavender always needs excellent drainage and full sun, whether in the garden or a pot.

Topiary

With careful pruning and shaping, lavender can be trained into a potted standard the same way as the more typical rosemary. Choose a perennial variety with a straight, woody center stem, and prune all other stems off the plant. As the plant continues to grow, cut out all side branches but allow the top to branch out. When the plant has reached the height you want, nip off the tip

Tender lavender in mixed pots of color can be easily moved in the garden for any occasion.

to encourage a more bushy habit. You can shear the leaves to a geometric form or let the plant grow naturally to allow it to bloom.

As with any lavender, good drainage is essential. Water when the soil is dry to the touch, fertilize minimally, and provide plenty of sunlight. If the trunk seems to be wandering off course as it grows, tie it to a small stake to train it upright. If you prefer a more natural, gnarled look, you can leave it unstaked, as a larger version of a traditional bonsai.

This potted plant will take several years to attain its full growth. You may keep it in a sunny area indoors year-round or let it summer on a patio or terrace and winter inside, to protect the roots from the cold. When I have a particularly lovely plant growing contentedly on my sunporch, I often use it for special occasions, such as a buffet centerpiece for a special party.

Bonsai

One spring, when I went to prune one of my old *angustifolias,* I found that the woody stem had become so bent and twisted that it reminded me of a cedar on a windswept coast. There was little top growth, and the plant looked like it might not make it another year. I dutifully pruned about one-fourth of the leaves and made a mental note to start a bonsai if this plant made it through the summer.

In August, the plant had grown and bloomed, and I was ready for my experiment. I lined a shallow bowl with plastic, and put down a layer of gravel and then some sandy soil. With a sharp pair of clippers, I pruned off most of the branching stems and top growth and clipped out much of the root structure as well. As with any bonsai, when pruning the roots to fit the shallow pot, you must keep a balance between root growth and top growth. The plant must not be top-heavy. Enough roots are needed to provide nourishment to whatever leaves (and flowers) you keep.

I planted the pruned lavender in the pot and put it in a sunny window, watering when dry and fertilizing lightly. After several weeks, all the old leaves had died back and new growth was sprouting from the woody stems. My elation was short-lived, however, as the plant died. My adventure over, I started a new bonsai with a young plant, following the recommended method so that the roots could adapt gradually to the restricted environment—a fine start for a young plant soon to grow into a classic bonsai.

Combinations

A single lavender plant makes little impact in the garden, as the blue-violet color of the flowers blends into the green foliage of other plants. The slender flower spikes are best viewed en masse. An older, well-pruned plant may make an impression, but it's most common to see lavenders planted in hedges or groups.

When combining lavenders with other plants in the garden, think of both the lavender flower and the foliage. Spring bulbs look wonderful with a backing of perennial lavender foliage. When other perennials are just starting to push their leaves aboveground, the gray, needlelike leaves of lavenders are already starting to put on a real show.

Here the lavender takes a backseat to the splashy gold coreopsis.

Lavender foliage looks fine almost any time of year in a mixed bed.

Lavender and violas are beautiful together. Later, incorporate annuals or place pots of color directly in the garden if bloom is important.

For a blue-purple garden, plant lavender with perilla and purple basils, globe thistle, verbenas, blue larkspur and delphinium, veronica speedwell, and a blue sage like 'Blue Bedder' or 'Victoria'. *Salvia argentia,* a sage with large, velvety, silvery leaves, enhances the gray color of the lavender leaves. Try purple pansies in spring and asters to highlight the second lavender bloom in late fall. Mix in white phlox or midsummer white lilies for contrast.

Combinations of lavender and pink are common, lavender and yellow less so. A gardener near me plants her lavender against goldenthread false cypress (*Chamaecyparis pisifera* c.v. *Filifera aurea*), and a designer at Longwood Gardens, in Kennett Square, Pennsylvania, chose a similar theme of lavender against dyer's woad *(Isatis tinctoria)*. I like to plant it with brilliant gold-orange heliopsis, golden yarrow, and globe centaurea.

Downy lavender *(L. multifida),* an annual in my garden, doesn't usually bloom until late July or August. By then the 3-foot-high spikes look great in combination with brilliant zinnias, never too ordinary for me to love.

When planning lavender combinations, consider when the flowers bloom in your area and how long the blooms last. If you are going to cut off the spikes for drying as soon as they begin to open, however, consider combinations of foliage rather than bloom sequences.

Moon Gardens

Even though the mogul emperor of India Jahan had a garden of white flowers and gray foliage planted in 1639 near Delhi, and perhaps others were planted before that, the modern reference for a moon garden is the restored garden at Sissinghurst, England, planted by Vita Sackville-West. That garden welcomes thousands of visitors a year, who are intrigued by the lovely bright white and gray plantings, shown to best advantage after dusk. The flowers reflect the moon's glow on summer evenings, and the pristine whiteness seems to shimmer on romantic evening strolls through the garden.

A moon garden is planted both for light and for fragrance, with narcissus, lilies, phlox, nicotiana, jasmine, and gardenias perfuming the air for the visitor. Lavender is often included because of its gray foliage and sometimes white flowers, which are perfect for a white theme garden.

To start a moon garden, select one bed or area of the garden, and choose plants that have white blooms and foliage that is white variegated or gray. The

This combination of pink coral bells and golden foliage sets off the purple to perfection.

gray color comes from the reflection of little hairs on the surface of the leaf and usually indicates that the plant is drought-tolerant, as the hairs protect the leaf from water depletion in the hot sun.

Decide whether you want to carry the white theme year-round or only in the summer. To enjoy a moon garden, plant it where you will sit on a summer evening, where you will stroll, or lacking time to do either, where you will stride in the evening to and from your home.

The plant lists for a white garden are endless, and it's fun to pore over the catalogs in midwinter and make your plans. Appropriate plants come in a variety of habits and species, including shrubs, climbers, annuals, and perennials.

Shrubs and Climbers

- Variegated lily-of-the-valley shrub, which has lovely green and white waxy foliage and drooping white panicles in May and June.

- A white rose like 'Fair Bianca', which has the form and scent of an old rose and has a second bloom.

- Gardenia, if appropriate to your planting zone.

- Hydrangea like 'Pee Gee' or the climbing hydrangea, both of which have large, dramatic blooms.

- Moonflower vine, an annual with huge, white, morning glory–like blooms that unfurl in the evening and die at dawn.

Perennials

- White lavenders are *L. angustifola* 'Melissa', which has a strong scent and a pink tinge, *L. a.* 'Alba', a white lavender, or *L. a.* 'Nana Alba', a dwarf white. Select by plant height and hardiness, and ask your favorite herb source for other recommendations.

- Lamb's ear, that velvety gray perennial.

- The bright, woolly 'Silver Sage' with its large, showy leaves.

- Babies' breath, which has a cloudy delicacy and never looks trite in the garden.

- White phlox, like the disease resistant 'Miss Lingard'

Early May at Longwood Gardens, in Kennett Square, Pennsylvania, finds the lavender still developing its leaves, but the stunning backdrop of dyer's woad and golden thread false cypress brightens things up considerably.

- One of the gray-white artemesias like the annual dusty miller or the perennials 'Silver King' or 'Silver Mound'.

- Goose neck loosestrife, if you can plant it in a contained area as it is an invasive but lovely summer bloomer.

Annuals

You may need to plant annuals from seed to get white selections, but look for "white" marigolds, 'zenith hybrid' zinnias, white snapdragons, nicotiana, cosmos, petunias, and alyssum. These will bloom all summer until frost and fill in your bed.

CHAPTER FIVE

Growing Lavender

*L*avender needs full sun; don't even think of planting it in your shade garden. Having said that, I know that there are gardeners who are determined to force their own stubborn will on a garden design regardless of the needs of the plants. I've seen stunted lavenders sparsely blooming under large trees, their spikes straining toward a stray beam of light. But life is hard enough without placing such a burden on your plants. If shrubs in mixed borders have grown up to shade the lavender almost completely, dig up the lavender and move it to a sunnier location.

Lavenders can stand a brief summer drought if they are established but should be watered if the drought is prolonged. Root rot is one of the few hazards of growing lavender. They won't tolerate standing in wet soil, and it's helpful to plant them in a raised bed, on a slope, or in a rock garden. In an herb garden bordered by bricks, the beds are often raised at least 6 inches to achieve better drainage. In general, the soil must be well drained and light so that the roots don't sit for a prolonged time in water. Add sand or pebbles to heavy clay or rich soils to lighten them. Lavender is considered to be moderately drought-tolerant and is one of the plants recommended for xeriscaping. It grows beautifully in many areas of the Southwest.

LEFT: A border of *L. a* 'Hidcote' and 'Munstead' plants, leading to the bookshop at Alloway Creek Gardens and Herb Farm, enjoys full sun.

If you insist on growing lavender in the shade, reconcile yourself to sparse bloom and spindly plants.

Soil should be on the alkaline side, though there is a latitude of pH 6.5 to 8.3. Some gardeners side-dress with pelletized lime in the spring. Recommendations are for average—not too rich—soil. An addition of compost or well-rotted manure to the top of the bed should be enough fertilizer for the year.

Fungus problems may occur if leaves remain damp. Keep young plants 2 to 3 feet apart to allow for good air circulation between plants; they will soon grow to fill in the space. Water in the mornings rather than the evenings so that the sun will dry off the leaves.

Horticultural Planting Zones

Lavenders are usually listed as hardy or tender. These categories refer to the ability of a plant to withstand frost. You can find out your horticultural zone by looking at the map appearing in most catalogs or by calling your county extension agent. If you want a perennial, select a plant that is hardy in your area. If you have a yen for one that is listed as tender, or you are north of the hardiness zone, treat the plant like an annual by planting it directly in the garden and saying good-bye at the end of the season, or plant it in a container that you overwinter indoors and set out again the next summer.

What the horticultural map can't tell you is the particular microclimate where you want to plant. In San Antonio, Texas, there is a difference of one whole zone between those plants growing near the famous river walk and those growing at street level, a few flights of steps above the river. The protection of the stone walls and the reflection of the warmth from the water make different plantings possible at the two levels.

If I'm not sure of the hardiness of a plant, I place it in a bed on the east side of my old stone farmhouse, where it is protected from the ever-present westerly winds and warmed by the radiation from the stone. South would be even better, but that's where my driveway is.

Zones are based on average temperatures, and some winters are above or below average in temperature and rainfall. During a recent mild winter, the warmest on record in northeastern Pennsylvania, some of the tender lavenders I had decided to treat as annuals survived. Snow may protect plants from heavy winds and from drying out. One extradry winter, I lost some azaleas that had done well for many years. Another winter, my perennial verbena decided to call it quits after several weeks of extraordinarily low temperatures. If you take a philosophical attitude when you lose a plant and view the loss as an opportunity for a design change rather than a tragedy, you can experiment with some plants on the borderline of your hardiness zone.

Attack the catalogs with a sense of humor and the attitude of a scientist performing an experiment, because there is often inconsistency between labels of seeds and plants, and even among catalogs. 'Lady' is listed as hardy in zones 5 to 8 in one catalog, 5 to 9 in another. Catalog copy that slipped past the editor's eye lists 'Lady' as hardy in zones 6 to 10 on one page and 5 to 9 on another. Still another catalog lists 'Lady' as tender. It can be confusing. But if you are in zone 3 or 4 and want a perennial lavender, try *L. angustifolia* 'Hidcote' or 'Munstead' in a sheltered location and insulate with a deep mulch. Too-rich soil tends to make the plants less winter hardy, so go easy on the fertilizer during the growing season.

A mulch or path of light stones reflects sunlight on the plants and helps prevent fungus diseases.

Humidity is more of a threat than heat, as lavender may succumb to fungus disease as one of its few problems. In humid areas, treat even hardy lavenders as annuals, and be prepared to replant every year as you would your tulip bulbs.

Pests and Diseases

If you want to mulch your lavender beds, avoid bark, hay, and shell mulches, which might retain too much moisture. The best mulch is a 2-inch cover of white sand or pebbles, which will reflect the sunlight back on the plant, hasten drying of rain or dew, and thus help prevent fungus diseases. You can also help prevent fungus problems by leaving some room for air circulation around your plants. The distance between plants will of course depend on the ultimate size of the plant; some shrubs will grow to as much as 5 feet across if they are happy with their situations. With a dwarf species, perhaps 12 to 18 inches across is the expected diameter. When you look carefully at photographs of the purple haze which represents commercial lavender beds you realize that while the shrubs may be touching down the row, they are mostly planted on raised beds and there might be 2 to 3 feet of air space between the rows.

Lavender seems to be unaffected by any insects or other pests, and gardeners on both coasts report that deer and gophers ignore the lavender plants as they enjoy the rest of the garden cafeteria. In fact, some gardeners believe that interplantings of lavender among more tasty species may help ward off deer.

One disease that kills lavender plants is shab. Spores of *Phoma lavandula* on the stem produce black spots, which will eventually kill the plant. It first causes the stems to turn brown. If you notice this on a sickly plant, pull it up and burn the plant, as there is no cure, and the spores can easily infect other plants. Wipe gardening clippers or other tools you have used on sick lavenders with alcohol before working your way around a garden bed, to avoid spreading infections.

Root rot is about the only other problem that your garden lavenders will face. Help prevent this problem by not overwatering and by waiting in the spring until the soil has warmed before setting out new seedlings.

Pruning

Prune in spring each year, after danger of hard frost, shaping the plant and lopping off about one-third of the top and sides. This process will encourage new growth and prevent the growth of woody and gnarled stems that make a five-year-old plant look ancient.

Drastically cutting an old plant back to the heavy wood may kill the plant, so it's better to be faithful about pruning from the first spring after

Mail-order nurseries sell uncommon cultivars that you may not find at local garden centers.

planting. If you do have an older plant that hasn't yet been pruned, approach the lavender with sharp clippers and a three-year plan. In spring when the first new growth is evident, cut about one-third of the stems back to within a few inches of where the woody part starts. Trim the rest of the stems back about one-third of the way. For the next two years, cut another third of the stems back near the wood and just trim all the remaining stems. In this way, you will prune the whole plant in three years without causing too drastic a shock to its system.

Buying Plants

Both seedlings and mature plants are available from local garden centers and by mail, from 4-inch pots to 1-gallon containers. Some sources are listed on pages 107 and 108. Experienced gardeners know that no matter how reliable the source, varieties may get mixed up or mislabeled. If your purchase is growing much taller than it should, or the leaves are wider than usual, you may have the wrong species. Nevertheless, you can still enjoy the plant for what it is.

You will pay more for larger plants than for seedlings, but you may decide it's worth it to get well-established plants, as young plants grow slowly. Since plants are usually propagated from cuttings in the nursery trade, check that there are roots established in a 4-inch pot and that you are not just buying a cutting freshly poked into the soil. Gently turn over the container and tap out the plant into your hand to check for visible roots. If there are none, wait a few weeks and try again, looking for plants that show growth at the tip of the branches.

Equally bad are seedlings with so many roots that when you take them out of the pot, the soil is completely covered with a mass of white threads. Pot-bound seedlings that have been left in the container too long are stressed and will have a difficult time when transplanted to the garden. If you do buy such a plant, take a pencil tip and gently tease out some of the roots before planting in the garden.

If you buy herbs or other plants at a supermarket or hardware store, you may get a wonderful buy and healthy plants if they were delivered to the store within the past day or two. Plants tend to be poorly cared for in such settings, however, and become very stressed after a couple days. Ask when the next delivery of herb plants comes in, and be there that day.

Even though I plant seeds of *L. angustifolia* under grow lights, they look rather pathetic until the second year. By then they're as sturdy as anything I can buy.

Starting from Seed

L. angustifolia can be grown from seed, but most seed companies warn customers that the results are somewhat variable. One packet of seeds will result in plants that are not totally uniform. If you want some plants to fill a few spots in your perennial beds, this may not be a problem, but if you want to plant a hedge, it might be best to keep the plants in a holding bed for a year to see what you've got before investing your efforts in what turns out to be an irregular border. Examine your plants after a year, and select those that are most similar to each other.

To confuse the issue, *L. angustifolia* seeds are also sold under the names English lavender, true lavender, *L. spica* (or spike lavender), *L. officinalis,* and *L. vera.* I asked one seed company why they are using old names on the seed packets, and the head horticulturist replied that they had an overabundance of printed packets and wanted to use them up before changing the name. No wonder gardeners are confused! If you want one of the cultivars, look for 'Hidcote', 'Munstead', or 'Lady'.

'Lady' was developed by Burpee and became an All-America Winner for 1994. It was touted as blooming the first year from seed, with a compact height of 12 inches, compared with the straight species listed at 30 inches, and appropriate for zones 5 to 9. I planted the seeds in doing my research for this book, and although the plants were small, they did indeed bloom in September of the first year.

Seeds should be started in flats in a soilless mix eight to ten weeks before the last frost date in your area. Stratify for three weeks by covering with plastic wrap and putting in a cold frame. Lacking a cold frame, I put some in an

After hardening off, plant hardy species in midspring, clustering plants with bulbs or perennials.

old refrigerator in my basement and some outside right next to a stone wall, covering the flat with boughs cut from a discarded Christmas tree. Both methods seemed to work, as the seeds showed a good rate of germination. After being removed from the cold frame, the seeds need light to germinate. I put mine on a windowsill. One tray that got overwatered did not tolerate the experience well and ended up on the compost heap.

As with all seedlings, harden them off by placing in a protected location out of full sun for about five days before planting out in the garden. Wait to plant until after the last frost date, and until the soil has warmed up a bit. Continue to water the first year, but make sure the drainage is good at the planting site so that the seedlings don't sit with wet feet for a prolonged period. Some experts suggest cutting off all flower spikes the first year as they start to develop, and long before full bloom, to put more strength back into the plant, but I confess that I let my lavender spikes bloom the first year, even if it takes more time for the plant to become fully established.

L. x *intermedia* cannot be grown from seed because it is a hybrid and is sterile. If you have visions of growing masses of 'Grosso', don't look for seed but plan on either taking cuttings from a friend or layering from a plant you already have.

Taking Cuttings

When you take cuttings from a mother plant, you know you will get plants identical to the mother, a cloning process. Another advantage is that you don't even have to own the mother. It's a rare friend or neighbor who won't generously offer you several pieces from her prized specimen if you make your wishes known. To sweeten the pot, why not offer some prize of your own in trade? Taking cuttings surreptitiously from a garden center or herb farm is not fair game, however tempting. Gardeners are among the most generous people, unless you swoop down in a public garden or on a home garden tour and pinch a piece into a plastic bag. A gardener who observes such behavior may come at you with hoe in hand.

To take a cutting, find a nice, small branch—approximately 6 inches—grasp the tip, and gently pull down to break off. The cutting must have a piece of the union or heel from the trunk of the plant in order to grow, so it's better to break off the piece than to cut it with clippers. Take off the lower leaves, but leave the upper ones. Stick the end in water, then dip in rooting powder. Make a hole in the ground with a dowel or fat twig, and stick the cutting in the hole, leaving only about 1 inch above ground.

Pauline Pettitt-Palenik of Cool Spring Lavender Farm on the Delmarva Peninsula, which is in zone 7, likes to take cuttings in the fall, when most of her other garden work is done. She places her cuttings in a cold frame and covers them on days of hard frost. Roots will develop and will continue their growth at the first signs of spring. At the end of the summer, her one-year-old plants are full and robust.

Those without cold frames, and lazy gardeners such as myself, prefer to take cuttings in mid- to late spring, when there is little chance of heavy frost. Keep watered but well drained until established. By the end of the summer, the plants will be smaller than those propagated from the same mother in the fall.

Propagating by Layering

In spring, start with one mother plant well established in your garden. Water the soil around the plant. Select an outside branch of pliable wood, and bend it gently to the ground. Measure 8 to 12 inches from the growing tip, and mark the spot on the ground where this point touches the earth. Strip the leaves and side branches off the branch you have chosen, leaving only about 6 inches of leaves at the tip. With a trowel, dig a small trench 3 to 4 inches deep at the site you have marked. *Rodale's Encyclopedia of Gardening* suggests wounding the stem at the burial point by making a small cut and inserting a toothpick at the wound site to keep it open. Dust the wound with rooting powder. Pin the wounded stem into the hole with a wire pin, and cover the area with soil. Stake the remaining branch tip with the leaves so that it stands upright. Water thoroughly, and keep watered and weeded. Check in the fall for root growth by gently removing soil from the area. Remove the anchoring pin and gently pull to feel if there is resistance from roots. If there is, cut from the mother plant but leave in place till the next spring, when it can be transplanted to a new site. If the branch hasn't rooted, don't make the cut, and recheck in the spring.

Plants at the Cool Spring Lavender Farm in Delaware enjoy sandy soil and good air circulation between rows.

Layering can be successful simply by bending down a branch and burying the middle part in dirt, without the wounding, dusting, and staking. In fact, some sprawling plants will layer themselves naturally and root without any assistance. These can be cut from the mother plant, left in place over winter, and transplanted in spring.

While you are layering and have all the materials at hand, it makes sense to try the technique with five or six branches. Think what a wonderful supply of new plants you'll have come spring.

CHAPTER SIX

Harvesting Lavender

Cutting for Drying

Whereas the French and English lavender farms that supply the perfume industry employ huge, mechanized equipment to cut lavender from the magnificent fields of blue, home gardeners and small flower and herb farms like mine use small hand shears to cut the spikes from their plants. In that way, home gardeners have an advantage, because not every spike on a plant ripens at the same time. We can be selective in harvesting, cutting one week, then the next, for optimal timing.

Cut when the spike has achieved full color and the first bud is starting to open. The flower will turn brown when it dries, so the spike will have better color if cut in the bud stage.

Cut spikes for drying when all the dew is off the flowers; late afternoon is a good time for the lavender. If that doesn't fit your schedule, cut anytime when the flowers are dry. How long to cut the stem depends on the use you have in mind. Cut down to near the bottom of the plant, including leaves, which also are fragrant, if you want a full bouquet to hang or you need long stems for a craft. The danger here is that you may also cut off some incipient

LEFT: Harvesting by hand from an acre of *L. x intermedia* 'Grosso' and 'Provence' at the Matanzas Creek Winery, Santa Rosa, California, for their annual lavender festival in June. PHOTO BY SANDRA MACIVER.

flower buds that would mature for a second harvest later in the summer. Cut down to the first leaf for most culinary purposes, if you want only buds for potpourri, or if you need only short stems for your craft designs.

Bunch the stems in small handfuls, bind with rubber bands, and hang with paper clips in a warm, dark, dry spot. As with any dried flower, the warmer, darker, and drier the atmosphere, the faster the bunch will dry and the better the color and fragrance will be preserved.

The bunch will dry in about a week. When fully dried, pack away in a cardboard box, and seal until you are ready to use your harvest in craft designs. The darkness will help keep the color from fading. For culinary lavender, seal in a plastic bag to keep the dust off.

Cut at their peak for drying, the flowers are still in the bud stage, when the color is strongest.

Small bunches wrapped with rubber bands and hooked with paper clips dry quickly in my hot attic in June and July.

Best Varieties for Drying

If you dry for decorative purposes, forget the pink and white lavenders. The colors that are lovely in the garden look dull and lifeless when dried. Forget *L. multifida* and *L. stoechas,* as the color is muddy. Buy plants with flowers of the deepest blue, like *L.* x *intermedia* 'Dutch' and *L. angustifolia* 'Hidcote', or plants that produce the longest, straightest stems, like *L.* x *intermedia* 'Grosso' or 'Provence'.

Cutting for Fresh Flowers

I have never seen fresh lavender sold in the wholesale flower markets of New York or Philadelphia. I've never seen fresh lavender sold in a florist shop, or even in a farm stand, and yet it makes a lovely cut flower. Granted, the stems are short, but a few handfuls picked in early bud will last for at least two weeks in a vase.

Cut the lavender early in the morning; dew is no problem to fresh flowers. Strip the bottom leaves, if any. Stand in water mixed with a commercial flower preservative according to package directions. You will have the joy of watching as the buds mature and the first flowers open, displaying a contrasting color to the buds. The fragrance is subtle, but as you walk by the vase, bruise a leaf or two to release more of the aroma.

Anyone can make a simple clustered arrangement. Fill small vases with any one species clipped from the garden.

On Display

Whether fresh or dried, lavender is a delightful flower to display in the home but is rather demanding in its usage. One principle I follow is to always use clusters of spikes in any design rather than using the stems singly. A single stem, though colorful and interesting if examined closely, gets lost surrounded by masses of other flowers.

Easy and Elegant Fresh Lavender

A large handful or two of cut fresh lavender in a crystal bowl needs no embellishment and sings its own praises by wafting a gentle aroma through the room. Sometimes, however, you have but a few stems of any one plant that you can spare from the garden. I love this small vase display because it works at almost any time of year, with different assortments of flowers and different numbers of containers. And even people untrained in floral design feel comfortable with the idea of shoving a few stems of a flower into a small vase. The late-spring display shown here features peonies, pansies, globe centaurea, bachelor's buttons, yarrow, lamb's ear, a purple bellflower, delphinium, and a few roses.

Even in late November and after several killing frosts, I can cull a few late mums, some cotoneaster berries, the silver leaves of santolina, a brave stem of delphinium growing in a sheltered location, some candytuft in rebloom, and a clipping or two of golden arborvitae for color, each in its own little container.

For containers, you can use egg cups, candlestick holders, sherry glasses, demitasse, sake or tiny teapots, or any other small containers that hold water. To go even smaller, I've even grouped eggshells or clustered chemistry lab test tubes on stands. When the containers are so small, it's important to top them up with water once or twice a day.

Easy and Elegant Dried Lavender

When using dried flowers and herbs, the number and assortment of potential containers increases dramatically. Without a water requirement, almost any object can be used to show off the flowers. The old baby shoes on the next page reflect the delicacy of the small flower buds of 'Dutch' lavender spikes. The stems are cut shorter to stuff into the high-topped shoes.

You can use a fabric or crocheted bootie in the same way, dipping it first in fabric stiffener mixed according to package directions (available in craft shops). Stuff it with waxed paper, and make sure it is standing upright on the sole so that it will hold its shape as it dries. A lineup of five or seven crocheted booties with lavender makes a delightful centerpiece for a baby shower, or you can give one to each guest as a party favor.

Fresh Flowers for Fragrance

A low bowl of fragrant flowers makes a perfect dining centerpiece, as it provides visual interest without interfering with the view of the guests around the table. When the lavender is budding and the flower spikes are ripening to full color, search the garden for other fragrant species. Do you have sweet peas, lily of the valley, or early roses? Gather whatever you have, along with other colorful blossoms. Condition the flowers by standing in a bucket of

Use unusual containers for dried materials.

Use some of your harvest for a big bowl of fresh lavender, which will last almost two weeks.

warm water for about ten hours. Then remove from the bucket and cut the stems short.

To help keep the flowers in place, make a grid with narrow adhesive tape or cellophane tape across the top of a china bowl. The bowl must be dry when you make the grid. Cross the bowl twice the long way and three times the short way. Make sure that the tape goes down the side of the bowl only about 1/2 inch so that it will not be visible when the leaves and flowers are in place. Edge the rim of the bowl with galax, ivy, or large violet leaves. Then add the other flowers in wild profusion.

CHAPTER SEVEN

Lavender Projects

Lavender Bundle

Traditional lavender wands use fresh lavender and weave ribbons in and out among the stems in such a way as to encase the flowers among the ribbons— a tidy way to have the scent without risking the dried buds dropping onto your linens. I have a confession to make: I've never made a lavender wand and likely never will. Because I'm never quite ready to sit down and weave my lavender stems when the flower spikes are ready to work with, and because I'm too lazy to go through the intricate process of weaving, and mostly because I love to see the purple-blue flower heads rather than hide them, I prefer to make lavender bundles. Place the bundle where it won't be frequently moved or handled, and you'll enjoy it for many years.

WHAT YOU NEED

two clusters dried lavender

two rubber bands

8-inch round lace doily

small bow

clippers

glue gun and glue sticks, thick white craft glue, or needle and thread

---

1. Put a rubber band around each cluster of dried lavender, and lay the clusters in the center of the doily, stems end to end. Trim the stems with clippers if they obscure the flowers on the other side. A bundle about 9 inches long should do nicely.

2. Bring up the two sides of the doily to make a tight wrap, and fold the edges back. Secure the center of the doily with a few drops of hot glue, craft glue, or a few stitches with needle and thread.

3. Attach a small bow in the center in the same way.

LEFT: A simple lavender bundle wrapped in lace can be displayed on a powder room shelf or used to scent a drawer.

Lavender Garland

This lavender garland can be made as long and as full as you wish, and because its base is a wire, you can make it any shape you wish: an elongated S curve to hang over a bed, an inverted U to drape over a mirror or picture, an L-shaped corner piece to frame the molding on a door or window, or a small M such as shown here. Modify the instructions below to suit the shape of your garland.

WHAT YOU NEED

16-gauge wire (from any hardware store)

wire cutters

hand clippers

florist's reel wire

lavender and other dried flowers, such as pearly everlasting globe amaranth, and love-in-a-mist

glue gun and glue sticks or thick white craft glue

bow (optional)

1. Cut the 16-gauge wire to the desired length, taking into account the extra wire needed for any curves, and bend it into the desired shape.

2. Plan ahead! For most shapes, you start to make the garland at one end of the frame and work toward the center. Upon reaching

This garland, used to adorn the graduation photos of two sisters, is small and delicate, but the same technique can be used to make massive arrangements.

the center, you bind off and start at the other end, again working toward the center. A bow or extra flowers will form the focal point at the center of the garland. If you want a continuous piece, start at one end and work all the way to the other.

3. For the small **M** shape shown here, tie the florist's reel wire to the bottom of one leg of the **M**. Take a small cluster of mixed flowers and lay them on the frame with the stems pointed upward, heads just past the bottom of the leg. Wrap tightly with reel wire once or twice to bind them in place.

4. Take another cluster of flowers and lay them on top of the stems of the first, hiding the stems, and bind them in place with wire. Continue this process, working up the leg of the **M**.

5. As you reach the corner, cut the stems shorter. Keep working across the top and down to the middle point of the end. After binding the last bunch, tie the wire securely in the back of the garland and cut off.

6. Tie the reel wire to the bottom of the other leg and repeat the above steps, meeting the other flowers at the top center.

7. Glue on extra flowers where necessary to hide stems and add fullness.

Meadow Sweet Wreath

In sunny Provence, France, where vast fields of lavender are planted to supply the perfume industry, bright blues and yellows are a favorite combination in home decor. The delicate wreath on the next page uses dried buttercups and wild mustard from the meadows near my home in Pennsylvania to complement the lavender-blue *L. angustifolia.* The base is made from wire, which means that you can make the wreath any size and shape, and for minimal cost.

1. To form the wreath base, measure enough 16-gauge wire to make a circle about 12 inches in diameter, and cut it from the roll. If you have a modest supply of flowers, start with a smaller wreath base.

2. Bend one end back 1 inch to make a hook. Slip the other end through and bend back to secure the circle.

WHAT YOU NEED

16-gauge wire (from any hardware store)

florist's reel wire, 22- to 26-gauge

hand clippers

wire cutter

dried lavender and other flowers

Dried lavender, wild buttercups, and mustard mix in this country-style herb wreath.

3. Make small bundles of dried lavender and other flowers, cutting the stems 8 to 10 inches long. Tie a piece of florist's reel wire to the wire frame, then start wrapping the bundles of flowers to the frame with the reel wire. The number of bundles you use will determine the fullness of the wreath.

French-Style Stacked Arrangement

The long, straight stems of lavender 'Grosso' give you just what you need for making a stacked arrangement. I have clustered the lavender to give it visual prominence, so that it doesn't disappear among the bold forms of the cockscomb and the cobra lily *(Saracenia)*. Those two flowers are striking as single stems. Note that cobra lily is a protected wildflower in some marshy areas. Either grow your own or buy fresh or dried from a reliable commercial source that is growing it for resale. It dries from the fresh state in about three days if bunched and hung in a warm, dark, dry spot. Other flowers with

This stacked, French-style arrangement is suitable for a most contemporary setting.

WHAT YOU NEED

basket or china bowl

one or two blocks of green floral foam (not Styrofoam, which is too stiff)

paring knife

hand clippers

green sheet moss

dried flowers, here lavender, cockscomb, cobra lily, and Queen Anne's lace

straight, sturdy stems work well in stacked arrangements, including larkspur, roses, globe thistle, yarrow, and safflower. For this design, it's best to use a container without a handle, here a 9-inch-square bamboo basket, but a beautiful square or rectangular china bowl also looks wonderful.

1. Fill the basket or bowl with foam from edge to edge, cutting and trimming as necessary with a paring knife, and cover the foam with sheet moss.

2. Start placing the flowers in the back row, four lilies and a cockscomb, all the stems cut to about 14 inches. Insert into the foam about 2 inches, spacing the flowers evenly.

3. In the next row, place four clusters of lavender. Each cluster has eight to ten stems and is slightly shorter than the back row.

4. Continue forward, each row an inch or so shorter than the row behind. Note that though I have varied the number of cobra lilies and cockscombs in a row, each of the rows of lavender has four clusters. Suit yourself in your design.

5. Finish off the edges with short flowers. Here I've used the delicate heads of Queen Anne's lace, which have been dried flat on a window screen.

Lavender Tower

This topiary tower, which can be used as a table arrangement or centerpiece, can be made with lavender alone or with a mix of dried flowers. Sometimes my choice is dictated by what I have on hand. Here I was in danger of using up my whole lavender supply, so I added pink and purple larkspur and golden touches of air-dried button mums.

1. To make an impressive, 20-inch tower, start with a 14-inch tall cone and cover with green sheet moss. Use floral pins to pin the moss onto the cone. Leave the bottom bare so that the tower will be stable.

A lavender tower can be used on a mantel or table, or wherever some drama is called for.

2. Start pinning small clusters of lavender, with the stems cut to about 8 inches, at the top of the tower. Allow the flower heads to extend above the point of the cone by 2 inches. Each cluster will have about ten stems. If you try to pin too many at one time, the pin will come loose.

3. Keep turning the tower as you go, working downward. When you reach 8 inches from the bottom, stop. Slip a sturdy rubber band over the cone, 3 inches from the bottom. Now, instead of pinning the clusters of lavender, slip the stems under the rubber band to hold them in place.

4. Tie several strands of raffia or a ribbon over the rubber band to hide it and give extra holding strength.

5. Now add extra stems of larkspur, mums, or other flowers in among the lavender, wherever it looks a little sparse. If you cut the stems fairly short, they need no extra pinning, as the lavender will hold them in place. Glue them in with hot glue if you desire.

Lavender Tree

Visitors to Meadow Lark Flower & Herb Farm were surprised to learn that this was last year's Christmas tree dressed in a different style. The tree had been left in a corner of the yard for almost a year, and all the needles had dropped off. Flat white spray paint completed the transformation.

Use your tree stand or, as here, insert the trunk into an old plastic pot weighted with rocks. Use foam insulator spray from the hardware store, following the directions on the can, to fill in the spaces between the rocks. This will harden completely in about an hour. Put the pot in a decorative jardiniere, and cover the base with green sheet moss.

The tree is decorated with posies of lavender tied with ribbon and tucked between the branches and with lavender displayed in cones. Add some bows in a similar ribbon, as well as some traditional tree ornaments in blues and lavenders. Here I tucked rose-colored statice between the branches to add more color.

This much-admired lavender tree, actually a recycled Christmas tree, was beautiful and fragrant.

Surprise a visitor by removing a cone of lavender from the tree and giving it as a gift.

You can buy metal cones or make your own using ice cream sugar cones from the supermarket. Spray with silver or gold paint, and glue on a small ribbon to serve as the handle.

If properly stored enclosed in a black plastic bag, the tree will last well from year to year. The dried lavender, statice, and sugar cones will also keep if carefully packed away. When removing from storage the next year, mist the dried flowers with water and let them sit for thirty minutes to make them less fragile to handle.

Lavender Lady

My garden displays usually include a scarecrow, more for decoration than utility, as they actually seem to encourage crows and other birds to make a feast of my scattered seeds. Nevertheless, they do enchant visitors to the garden, both big and small, and maintain a long tradition. This scarecrow was named for Burpee's 'Lady', a variety of *L. angustifolia* that blooms from seed the first year.

WHAT YOU NEED

two broomsticks or dowels

twine

hay

gourd

saw

hand clippers

clothing: long-sleeved dress, leotard, man's T-shirt, hat, boots

My Lavender Lady sports a dress dyed for the occasion, and if her head seems rather small, it's because the drought year kept my gourds from achieving the size I aimed for. She must spend the summer minding the lavender patch and thinking small thoughts. This lady was designed to sit on a hay bale or an old wooden reel. The wooden reels that once held electric cable are often free for the taking. Call your local electric company to find out.

1. Measure the width of the dress across the shoulders, and cut one broomstick or dowel to that size.

2. Place the cut shoulder piece across the uncut broomstick, 12 inches down from the top, to form a cross. Use some twine to bind the two broomsticks together securely.

3. Put the T-shirt over the shoulders and stuff with hay. Slip on the leotard and stuff with hay. Make a small hole in the leotard so that the stick can

My Lavender Lady enjoys herself too much in my cutting garden to actually scare away any critters.

poke down through them as the legs bend into a sitting position. Tie the leotard to the T-shirt at the waist with twine.

4. Put on the dress and stuff the sleeves with more hay. Bind the wrists with twine.

5. Cut a hole in the gourd and put it over the top stick to form the head. You may want to add a neck scarf to cover the exposed stick.

6. Slip on the boots and hat. Does a lavender lady carry a purse? These and other fashion questions you must decide yourself.

CHAPTER EIGHT

Lavender Potpourris

The word *potpourri* means a stew, a mixture, a medley, or a collection, and it is most popularly used to refer to a glorious mixture of scented botanicals that please the eye and perfume the home.

In the commercial marketplace, there is a huge variation in prices and esthetics of potpourris, as dyed wood shavings may replace dried flowers and herbs to bring down the cost, and artificial scents often add a harsh or cloying note to the aroma. Though lavender buds are used in many commercial potpourris as part of the mixture, their delicate scent is often overpowered by chemical fragrances. If I'm taking the time and effort to bake a cake, I use butter, never margarine, to get the most flavorful results. My theory is make every calorie count. So it is with potpourris: The finest ingredients produce fabulous results.

When you make your own potpourri, you have the agreeable task of combining pure and delightful ingredients, and the very act of mixing the "stew" is a pleasure. Some prefer to combine all the ingredients and then dole out the mixture into bowls and packs for gift giving, with one or two special flowers on top. Others prefer to meticulously arrange their potpourris in layers and rows.

Before you start, think of four basic needs for any potpourri: aroma, color, texture, and longevity, or keeping quality. Aroma is an absolute necessity, but

LEFT: This potpourri features the classic color combination of blue and gold, as well as the classic scent of lavender.

the others are not. You can keep your mixture in a lidded porcelain jar with holes to let the scent escape while hiding the contents. You can stir and bruise your potpourri weekly to release additional scent, add a few drops of essential oils as the original scent begins to fade, or make a new potpourri every six months. To many, mixing a new potpourri is a treat.

The longevity of potpourris, and dried flowers and herbs in general, has been vastly exaggerated by commercial interests. Any arrangement or mixture should be tossed after two years at the maximum, if only to get rid of the dust accumulation. I just visited my attorney's office about a business matter and spied in his conference room a once lovely arrangement that I had sent when he moved into new quarters about eleven years ago. Although there was a semblance of color remaining, the structure was mostly intact, and the frosted glass vase was still elegant, I had to restrain myself from tossing the arrangement in the trash.

Lavender and rose potpourri can be displayed in a carefully designed pattern rather than in the traditional mixed form.

Aroma

Favorite scents are individualistic, based on both biology and learning. Special scents from childhood that evoke pleasant memories are particularly powerful. A whiff of summer phlox always evokes a memory of myself at three years old with a favorite uncle in a summer garden.

Some potpourri makers use essential oils to contribute most or all of the fragrance and concentrate on color and texture in the recipe. I prefer to use as little essential oil as possible, adding it only when I want a scent that is not otherwise available, such as patchouli or sandalwood.

Use lavender to add a sweet fragrance. Other recommended sweet smells are rose, lemon verbena, rose geranium, mountain mint, sweet annie, heliotrope, lily of the valley, peony, and gardenia. For pungent and spicy smells, try bergamot, pinks and carnations, cloves, nutmeg and cinnamon, eucalyptus, orange lemon and grapefruit rind, curry plant, tansy and yarrow, sage, juniper, spruce and other conifer needles, star anise, patchouli, sandalwood.

Texture

Add texture to your potpourri by using some choice botanicals that may not have any aroma but are interesting to look at and touch; they will make a nice contrast to the more delicate dried blossoms and petals. Using a few whole flowers in mixtures that are mostly broken pieces or petals also contributes immensely to visual appeal. Try air-dried roses on top of a potpourri of mostly rose petals, or dried heads of Queen Anne's lace on top of any floral or woodsy combination.

Some good botanicals for texture are small conifer cones, whole or in petals; small pods, such as love-in-a-mist and Oriental nigella; rose hips; pussy willow catkins; juniper and other dried berries; Kentucky coffee beans; Job's tears or other large seeds; small clusters of hydrangea flowers; leaves and buds of lamb's ear; and any whole dried flower with an interesting shape.

Color

Many cheap mixtures combine color indiscriminately, but the most beautiful potpourris are often those with botanicals that stick to a particular color palette or blend into one color range. In one of the potpourri recipes given

A combination of rose heads and petals complement the lavender in this concoction.

later in this chapter, the rich blue bachelor buttons and blue hydrangea clusters are added for color and texture, though they add no aroma to the mixture. The lamb's ear has a slightly bluish cast and a velvety texture that's hard to resist.

Also try adding opposite colors. The golden orange of calendulas, for example, is opposite on the color wheel from the blues and purples of the other materials and will add a cheerful note to your potpourri.

Fixatives

Most recipes call for a fixative to help keep the aromas of the potpourri from dissipating too quickly. They often contribute a fragrance of their own, thus adding in a second way to the mixture. One of the fixatives most commonly included is orris root, which is the root of the Florentine iris, dried and finely chopped or ground into a powder. If you can't find it anywhere else, ask a

pharmacist to order it for you. The chopped form is better to use for potpourris, as the powder of orris root, as well as cinnamon, another fixative, will
coat the rest of the ingredients with a light film.

Other aromatic fixatives are the whole forms of vanilla beans, cloves, nutmeg, and cinnamon stick pieces. Penny Black, in *The Book of Potpourri*, also
lists chamomile flowers, coriander seeds, angelica, sweet cicely, cumin, and
the dried leaves of lemon verbena and sweet woodruff as other easy-to-find
fixatives. So when orris root is listed in a recipe, don't be afraid to substitute.

To make a dry potpourri, Black recommends mixing essential oils and any
spices or heavily aromatic materials with the fixative and rubbing the mixture
with your fingers before adding the petals and flowers and other materials.
She also suggests letting the mixture age in a tightly covered container for six
weeks to achieve the longest-lasting results.

Potpourri Recipes

Here are three of my favorite recipes, using lavender as a main ingredient.
With any potpourri recipe, you can add or substitute any of your own favorite
flowers, leaves, or aromatics.

PURELY LAVENDER

1. Mix the lavender buds with the essential
   oil and place in a decorative container.

2. Place your best dried rose in the center
   and the rosebuds and petals in a pattern
   around the mixture.

3. To refresh and release more aroma as the weeks go by, gently reach in and
   bruise the lavender buds with your thumb and fingers, stirring gently so
   as not to disturb the rose pattern.

INGREDIENTS

3 cups lavender buds

3 drops lavender essential oil

1 cup rosebuds and rose petals

BRIDAL POTPOURRI

Many brides wish to preserve their bouquets, centerpieces, and other wedding
flowers but think of it only when on their honeymoon. A phone call to mom
from a faraway destination often prompts a phone call to me or another
expert who preserves special flowers. When the flowers are two days old or
older, I can never capture the once-magnificent look of the flowers. There are

In this bridal potpourri, the whole lilies and lilacs from the wedding bouquet are for show. Tiny buds of lavender have little visual impact, but their fragrance is notable.

three solutions: buy replacement flowers and dry the new and perfect flowers, toss them in the compost heap, or make a wedding potpourri.

To make a wedding potpourri, I like to use a decorative bowl or dish from the household treasury, perhaps a family keepsake or antique, or something new from the wedding gifts.

1. Take apart the bride's bouquet and any other flowers still available— a centerpiece, bridesmaids' flowers, altar flowers. Hang the flowers in small bunches or lay them flat on window screens to air-dry. Most foliage I sandwich between sheets of newspaper and place under my dining room rug to dry.

2. When the drying is complete, sort through the materials and set aside the nicest ones. These will probably be the roses, fern, ivy, baby's breath, heather, larkspur, and any other flowers that air-dry well. Discard any brown and disgusting-looking things.

3. To the reserved flowers, petals, and leaves, add 1/2 cup of lavender buds and enough other aromatics from your own collection to make 4 cups.

4. Add a fixative (see page 94), as well as 5 or 6 drops of an essential oil in a scent to match the flowers or the season of the wedding—lily of the valley, lavender, or rose for spring or summer, or one of the spicier scents for fall or winter.

5. Decorate the top of the bowl with whole flowers.

I'VE GOT THE BLUES

This is a simple mixed potpourri of dried blue flowers with contrasting touches of orange.

1. Mix the essential oils with the lavender buds. Cover and let age for several weeks.

2. Mix in all the other dried flowers. Dress the top of the bowl with whole sunflowers, dahlias, or zinnias.

INGREDIENTS

2 cups lavender buds

2 cups bachelor's button flowers

2 cups blue hydrangea clusters

2 cups lamb's ear buds

1 cup calendula flowers

whole sunflowers, dahlias, or zinnias to decorate top

4 drops lavender essential oil

3 drops patchouli essential oil

CHAPTER NINE

Cooking with Lavender

Lavender is a member of the mint family with a lovely scent and a unique flavor. Some of the many species have distinctive tastes that have been incorporated into cooking. In the Provence region of France, lavender may be selected for a *bouquet garni* of *herbes de Provence,* a bundle of herb sprigs tied with a string for easy removal from the pot. The *fines herbes* traditionally include parsley, chives, tarragon, thyme, and chervil, to which are added one or more stems of basil, fennel, sage, saffron, or lavender. The flavor of the herbs is designed to enhance the main ingredients and shouldn't dominate the dish.

The aroma of the flower is a good indication of whether you will like the flavor. Some lavenders veer toward the camphorous, but the *angustifolias* are sweet in both aroma and taste. My favorite for cooking is 'Hidcote', a variety that is commonly grown in gardens in the United States and England.

As with any edible flower or herb, any lavender you plan to eat must be clean and pesticide free. That means knowing the source—either harvesting from your own or a friend's organic garden or buying from a reliable commercial grower of edible herbs. Farms that grow lavender for perfume or decoration don't adhere to the same standards of purity that you want for food. Though lavender is not a plant that attracts insect pests, and thus probably doesn't need spraying, always know what you are using in your cooking.

A little goes a long way when using lavender in cooking. If 1/2 teaspoon of dried lavender imparts a subtle and delicious flavor, 3 teaspoons in the same

LEFT: Sweet and savory foods can be enhanced by a touch of lavender.

dish may be overwhelming. You can use fresh or dried lavender in your recipes, but as with other herbs and spices, dried lavender buds have more than double the power of the fresh herb, as the flowers shrink when drying and the oil is concentrated. To release the oils of any herb in cooking, gently bruise between your fingers before dropping it into the pot.

Lavender is used to flavor sugar, jellies, cakes, and puddings. The flowers are also used in salads and savory dishes like beef stews and pot roasts. A little dried orange rind imparts a wonderful flavor combined with the lavender in these dishes. I've also seen mustards flavored with lavender, honey, and mint. You can use the young leaves as well as the flowers in cooking, and if you are making herbal vinegars, the leaves add some visual appeal to the spikes in the bottle.

A flavorful trick for barbecuing is to throw a few dried branches of lavender on the coals during the last few minutes of grilling chicken or fish, the way you might with rosemary or other herbs. The oils impart a delicious flavor that your guests might not recognize immediately, but they are bound to ask you about it.

For wonderful little gifts, save small, capped spice bottles, remove the old labels, and fill with your own dried lavender buds. Affix a new label and attach a copy of your favorite lavender recipe with a little gold string.

Aromatic Chicken

Here's a quick, flavorful main dish for company or for the family. The aroma while cooking and the taste thereafter will bring a smile to your face. The fat count is low and the eating is healthy. Orange zest is the colored skin removed from the bitter white part just below. Use a sharp knife or vegetable peeler to cut strips of this outer layer of the orange. For this recipe, it needn't be even and pretty.

INGREDIENTS

3 whole chicken breasts, skinned and split, or 6 thighs with legs attached, skinned

1 tablespoon butter

1/2 pound baby white onions, peeled

1/2 cup dry white wine

3 cloves garlic

1/2 teaspoon dried lavender buds

3 strips orange zest

salt and pepper to taste

Melt butter and sauté chicken in a nonstick pan. Brown on both sides. Add baby onions and brown quickly. Add the rest of the ingredients and cover pan. Simmer gently for 30 minutes. Remove garlic cloves and strips of orange. Serve over boiled rice or couscous. Garnish with whole orange sections and sprigs of fresh lavender. Serves 6.

Herbed Potato Salad

A tasty but low-fat contribution to a cookout or picnic is always appreciated. Rather than using low-fat mayonnaise, I substitute yogurt, which imparts both moisture and tang to the dish.

Boil unpeeled potatoes till soft but not mushy. Drain and let cool. Slice with skin or cut in half, depending on size; leave small ones whole. Mix the herbs and seasonings with the yogurt, and gently stir into the potatoes. Garnish with the edible flowers. Refrigerate till serving time. Serves 6.

INGREDIENTS

3 pounds flavorful small potatoes, like Red Bliss or Yukon Gold

1 cup low-fat plain yogurt

2 cups chopped young lovage or celery with leaves

1/2 cup chopped chives or green scallions

1 tablespoon fresh lavender flowers or 1/2 tablespoon dried buds

salt and pepper to taste

2 tablespoons Dijon-style mustard

1/2 cup borage flowers, calendula, chive, dill, or other edible flowers, and purple basil leaves for garnish

Lavender adds a surprising flavor to a light potato salad.

INGREDIENTS

hot, sterile bottle with screw lid or stopper,
  to hold approximately 8 ounces

white vinegar

funnel

2 stems purple basil

2 stems lavender

1 stem rosemary

6 fat blueberries

Lavender Vinegar

Pour the vinegar into the bottle using the funnel. Fill almost to the top. Cut the herb stems so that they will fit upright in the bottle. Drop in the washed blueberries and the stems of washed herbs. Cap and let steep two weeks before using, shaking occasionally. Label as desired. The purple basil will infuse the vinegar with a rosy glow. Refrigerate.

INGREDIENTS

6 medium to large tart apples, like Granny Smith
  or Winesap

1/4 cup lemon juice

1/2 cup honey

1 1/2 cups dry red wine

1/4 cup cassis (optional)

1/2 teaspoon vanilla extract

2 black peppercorns

1/4 teaspoon nutmeg

1/4 teaspoon cardamom

1/2 teaspoon dried lavender buds

1 cup raisins, golden or dark

Poached Apples

This easy recipe is low-fat and is sweet but refreshing. Substitute pears for apples in fall and winter, and try plums or peaches in the summer for a pleasing variation. You can also mix in whatever other fruits you have. A last-minute addition of fresh pink grapefruit or navel orange sections to the apples imparts a contrasting cool tartness to the cooked fruit.

Halve, peel, and core apples. Place face-down in a 10- to 12-inch skillet. Mix all other ingredients together and pour over apples. Bring just to a boil, reduce heat, cover, and simmer. Check with a fork after 15 minutes to see if apples are tender; if not, cook 5 to 10 minutes longer. If left too long, you will have delicious applesauce to pour over ice cream. Remove apples and raisins from skillet with a slotted spoon to a serving dish. Boil the remaining liquid for a few minutes to reduce and thicken. Pour over apples and let cool. Garnish with fresh lavender or other edible flowers, if available. Serve alone or with ice cream, whipped cream, or frozen yogurt. Serves 6.

Crystallized lavender, roses, and calendula decorate a creamy lemon tart for a very special occasion.

Crystallized Lavender for Decoration

Lavender and other flowers can be crystallized to decorate a special tart or cake. Once they were considered to be edible, but with today's cautions about eating raw egg, it's best to use them for decoration only. Even so, it's wise to use edible flowers, even if you aren't going to eat them. Small roses and lavender are favorites, along with lavender leaves. You can prepare these colorful flowers, herbs, and leaves at least a week ahead to adorn a wedding cake or other party dessert. Kids who don't mind messy fingers will love to help you. If you are pressed for time, forget the crystallizing and just use your blooms fresh from the garden.

INGREDIENTS

superfine granulated sugar

1 egg white mixed with 1 tablespoon of water

sheet of waxed paper

new small paintbrush

teaspoon

assortment of fresh flowers and leaves

Rinse off the flowers and herbs to remove soil and insects, shake, and let dry on the counter for 30 minutes. Use a fork to beat the egg white with the water. Paint a flower stem with the egg white mixture, covering front, back, and between the petals. Pour some sugar onto a plate. Roll the flower around in the sugar. Use the teaspoon to pour sugar into hard-to-reach places. Gently shake off excess sugar. Put the flower on a sheet of waxed paper and leave overnight for the sugar to dry. If you used too heavy a hand with the egg white, sprinkle more sugar on with a spoon to absorb it. When the sugar seems dry, store flowers in a single layer in a lidded container until ready to use.

Lemon Loaf Lavandula

I took this loaf as my contribution to a covered dish supper of a gardening group in New York City and asked for comments. Some tasters couldn't identify the herb but claimed it was delicious. Others thought at first it needed a smidgen more lavender, as the taste buds adapted to the flavor by the end of the slice. Someone else thought the flavor got more intense as she kept eating. I think cooks should please themselves, and for me, a hint of something wonderful is best. This moist, delicious tea or dessert loaf has a subtle lavender flavor. For a more intense flavor, add no more than another 1/2 teaspoon dried buds to the creamed mixture.

Heat the oven to 325 degrees. Grease a 9-by-5-by-3-inch loaf pan. Cream the butter and sugar until soft. Add the eggs one at a time, beating until smooth. Add the rind and lavender. Combine the flour, baking soda, and salt, mixing lightly with a spoon. Add the dry ingredients and the milk into the creamed mixture, alternating in two or three pours. Beat until just mixed. Don't overbeat. Pour batter into greased loaf pan and smooth top with a knife. Bake for about an hour, or until a toothpick inserted into the center of the loaf comes out clean.

INGREDIENTS

Cake

1/3 cup butter

1 cup sugar

2 eggs

1 tablespoon grated lemon rind

1 teaspoon dried lavender buds
 (off the stem; no leaves)

2 1/2 cups sifted flour

1 tablespoon baking powder

1/2 teaspoon salt

1 cup milk

Glaze

1/2 cup sugar

1/2 cup fresh lemon juice

1/2 teaspoon lavender

1 tablespoon grated lemon rind

A favorite for teatime or dessert, lemon loaf lavandula travels well, slices neatly, and tastes sensational.

Toward the end of the baking period, combine glaze ingredients in a small pan, bruising the lavender between your fingers before adding it. Bring to a boil, stirring constantly, and when the sugar is all dissolved, remove from stove. Prick the top of the loaf all over with a toothpick. Pour the glaze slowly over the top of the loaf until it is all absorbed. When the loaf cools a little, remove from pan. It's best to let it sit for 10 to 12 hours before slicing.

Lavender Sources

Lavender Plants

Cool Spring Lavender Farm
RD 2
Milton DE 19968
302-684-8325
Landscape-size plants, bed & breakfast, tours by appointment

Goodwin Creek Gardens
PO Box 83
Williams, OR 97544
541-846-7357
Many species and varieties of lavender plants and seeds

Nichols Garden Nursery
1190 N. Pacific Highway NE
Albany, OR 97321-4580
541-928-9280
Catalog, plants, and seeds

Sandy Mush Herb Nursery
316 Surrett Cove Rd.
Leicester, NC 28748-5517
Send $6 for catalog (deductible from order)

Well-Sweep Herb Farm
205 Mt. Bethel Rd.
Port Murray, NJ 07865
908-852-5390
Extensive list of more than sixty hardy and tender varieties, catalog, tours and classes by appointment

White Flower Farm
PO Box 50
Litchfield, CT 06759-0050
800-503-9624
Full-color catalog, enjoyable to read

LEFT: 'Lady', grown from seed, celebrating its second birthday with the shrub rose 'Ferdy'.

Lavender Seeds

W. Atlee Burpee Co.
300 Park Ave.
Warminster, PA 18974
800-888-1447

Thompson & Morgan
PO Box 1308
Jackson, NJ 08527-0308
800-274-7333

Dried Lavender

Meadow Lark Flower & Herb Farm
Ellen Spector Platt, Proprietor
RD 1 Box 1568
Orwigsburg, PA 17961
717-366-1618
Lavender by the bunch, lectures and group tours of farm by appointment

The Herb Lady
PO Box 2129
Sheperdstown, WV 25443
304-876-9435
Buds by the pound for potpourris, essential oils, wholesale and retail catalogs

Purple Haze Lavender Farm
180 Bell Bottom Rd.
Sequim, WA 98382
360-683-1714
U-pick fresh lavender

Matanzas Creek Winery
6097 Bennett Valley Rd.
Santa Rosa, CA 95404
707-528-6464
Winery with extensive estate-grown lavender plantings, handmade lavender products, self-guided tours, early-summer lavender festival

Other Sources of Interest

Mary E. Vogel
Lavender Hedge
8 Harvard Circle
Norristown, PA 19401
610-279-8372
Tours and talks by appointment from a lavender expert

Alloway Creek Gardens and Herb Farm
Barbara A. Steele, Proprietor
456 Mud College Rd.
Littlestown, PA 17340
717-359-4548
Annual Lavender Tea Party with herbal crafts and a Lovely Lavender Day, as well as a variety of herb plants for sale

Herb Research Foundation
303-449-2265
Natural Healthcare Hotline for updated information on herbs and herbal products, including safety, dosage, and contraindications. There is a charge for the call.

Further Reading

Bender, Richard W. *Herbal Bonsai: Practicing the Art with Fast-Growing Herbs.* Mechanicsburg, PA: Stackpole Books, 1996.

Black, Penny. *The Book of Potpourri.* New York: Simon & Schuster, 1989.

Bradley, Fern Marshall, and Barbara W. Ellis, eds. *Encyclopedia of Organic Gardening.* Emmaus, PA: Rodale Press, 1992.

Dodt, Colleen K. *The Essential Oils Book.* Pownal, VT: Storey Communications, 1996.

Duke, James A. *The Green Pharmacy.* Emmaus, PA: Rodale Press, 1997.

———. *Medicinal Plants of the Bible.* New York: Trado-Medic Books, 1983.

Gerard, John. *The Herbal; or General History of Plants.* London: John Norton, Publisher, 1597.

Grieve, Mrs. M. *A Modern Herbal.* 2 vols. New York: Dover Publications, 1931, 1971.

Hemphill, John and Rosemary. *What Herb Is That?: How to Grow and Use the Culinary Herbs.* Mechanicsburg, PA: Stackpole Books, 1997.

Kirkpatrick, Debra. *Using Herbs in the Landscape: How to Design and Grow Gardens of Herbal Annuals, Perennials, Shrubs, and Trees.* Mechanicsburg, PA: Stackpole Books, 1992.

Kowalchik, Claire, and William H. Hylton. *Rodale's Illustrated Encyclopedia of Herbs.* Emmaus, PA: Rodale Press, 1987.

Krutch, Joseph Wood. *Herbal.* Boston: David R. Godine Publisher, 1976.

Northcote, Lady Rosalind. *The Book of Herb Lore.* New York: Dover Publications, 1971. (Originally published in 1912 under the title *The Book of Herbs.*)

Platt, Ellen Spector. *Flower Crafts: A Step-by-Step Guide to Growing, Drying, and Decorating with Flowers.* Emmaus, PA: Rodale, 1993.

————. *How to Profit from Flower and Herb Crafts.* Mechanicsburg, PA: Stackpole Books, 1996.

————. *Natural Crafts from America's Backyards: Decorate Your Home with Wreaths, Arrangements, and Wall Decorations Gathered from Nature's Harvest.* Emmaus, PA: Rodale, 1997.

————. *The Ultimate Wreath Book: Hundreds of Beautiful Wreaths to Make from Natural Materials.* Emmaus, PA: Rodale, 1995.

————. *Wreaths, Arrangements, and Basket Decorating: Using Flowers, Foliage, Herbs, and Grasses to Make Colorful Crafts.* Emmaus, PA: Rodale, 1994.

Sheldon, Elisabeth. *A Proper Garden: On Perennials in the Border.* Mechanicsburg, PA: Stackpole Books, 1989.

Index